DRAWING FROM TEN YEARS OF CLOSE FRIENDSHIPS AND CORRESPONDENCES WITH MANY OF HER SURVIVING IDOLS, DOCUMENTARY FILMMAKER AND WRITER LIZ GOLDWYN INVITES US TO STEP BACK INTO AN ERA WHEN THE HOURGLASS FIGURE WAS IN VOGUE AND STRIPTEASE WAS A TRUE ART FORM.

Praise for Liz Goldwyn and *Pretty Things*

"Goldwyn's amazing book not only reinforces my lifelong fascination with those glorious goddesses of tease, but proves the old girls could certainly teach today's plastic, inflated cuties a thing or two about the mysteries of sex appeal."
—Bob Mackie, fashion designer

"Burlesque is in the eye of the beholder, anywhere from dispassionate to lascivious. Come what may, Liz Goldwyn takes the high road, in good taste, truthful and humane."
—Albert Maysles, documentary filmmaker

"A labor of love, and visual cornucopia, devoted to the golden era of a lost art. Liz Goldwyn's enthusiasm for her burlesque queen sisters is captivating."
—Richard Ziegfeld, grandson of Florenz Ziegfeld and author of *The Ziegfeld Touch*

"What fabulous women. I know now I missed my true calling."
—Sue Mengers, Hollywood legend

"Liz Goldwyn captures the end of an era in American entertainment, when the art of seduction was at its finest. Carefully researched and opulently illustrated, this book provides an insightful history of the tease and the women who understood its power of illusion."
—Tiffany Dubin, founder of Sotheby's fashion department and author of *Vintage Style*

"Liz Goldwyn writes with the passion and authority of a true devotee. *Pretty Things* is a marvelous tribute to the weird and wonderful world of burlesque."
—Bryan Ferry, musician

Pretty Things

THE LAST GENERATION OF AMERICAN BURLESQUE QUEENS

Liz Goldwyn

DEY ST.
AN IMPRINT OF
WILLIAM MORROW *PUBLISHERS*

A hardcover edition of this book was published in 2006 by HarperCollins Publishers.

HarperCollins books may be purchased for educational, business, or sales promotional use.
For information please write: Special Markets Department, HarperCollins Publishers,
195 Broadway, New York, NY 10007.

FIRST IT BOOKS EDITION PUBLISHED 2011.

The Library of Congress has cataloged the hardcover edition as follows:
Goldwyn, Liz.
Pretty things : the last generation of American burlesque queens /
Liz Goldwyn ; edited by Jennifer Augustyn ; art direction by Frank Longo. —1st ed.
p. cm.
Includes bibliographical references and index.

ISBN-13: 978-0-06-088944-9
ISBN-10: 0-06-088944-6
1. Burlesque (Theater)—United States—History. I. Augustyn, Jennifer. II. Title.

PN1942.G66 2006
792.70973—dc22
2006041817

ISBN 978-0-06-201181-7 (pbk.)

20 21 SCP 10 9 8 7 6 5 4

IN MEMORY OF

Anita Arden

Athena the Grecian Siren of Sex

Candy Barr

Sherry Britton

Red Buttons

Richard Collier

Blaze Fury

Gussie Gross

Margie Hart

Anita Middleton

Fayard Nicholas

Rozell Rowland

June St. Clair

Tana the Persian Princess

Tanayo

Joan Torino

Zorita

BRA
SLIP
PANTS
STRING

FOREWORD

BETTY ROWLAND

In light of Liz Goldwyn's film, *Pretty Things,* and now her book by the same title, I'm so glad that I met this visionary young woman, years ago, at the lovely home of burlesque costume designer supreme, Gussie Gross. In fact, it seems that we were destined to meet, as I had had a "confrontation" with her grandfather, Samuel Goldwyn, back in my "Ball of Fire" days, long before the author of this book was born.

Over the past several years, Liz's fascination with costumes and stripteases has led her to many characters along the way, including me. Our interviews were always a pleasure and her interest in the people in the burlesque field brought back so many memories of old times, and of my sisters Dian and Rozell, who would have enjoyed knowing Liz, too. I miss them so, and it moves me to tears to see them acknowledged and honored in this book.

What makes Liz special as a young connoisseur of burlesque is her own willingness to wear the costumes and learn the art. Although Liz had a few pratfalls in preparing her own striptease act (which come with the territory, as it takes four shows a day to perfect an act), she was a good student. Her enthusiasm is contagious and I am happy to be part of this book, contributing an insider's view of the real world of burlesque—both on and off the stage. Though we performers were working hard, making a living, and entertaining the public, society in general considered burlesque to be a dirty topic, and being a burlesque queen certainly had its ups and downs.

However, Liz Goldwyn's youthful perspective and desire to see the glamour in our past lives shine a new light on the subject. The charisma and energy she has poured into this book does justice to all the talented people who appear in these pages, and I am sure that *Pretty Things* would have inspired great joy in those who are no longer with us.

PROLOGUE

As long as I can remember, I have been spellbound by secondhand garments. I am convinced that every garment holds undiscovered revelations about its past lives.

Spirits haunt old ball gowns, spare gloves, and faded velvet corsages—their voices speak to me, recalling more romantic times.

My grandmother, Frances Howard, was a silent film actress and a model for *Vogue* in the 1920s. While Edward Steichen's photographs captured her look for posterity, sadly, none of her personal wardrobe survived. My grandfather, Samuel Goldwyn, a movie producer known for his taste and attention to detail, once hired Coco Chanel to make wardrobes for his stars. Her costumes were never used because, at the time, Hollywood actresses wanted gowns that would emphasize their curves. They were horrified by Chanel's androgynous "chic." When I asked my father where these Chanel costumes might be stored, he recalled last seeing them "in a garbage bag on a loading dock at the studio." Sadly, they were long gone and barely recorded. I pined for these mementos of the past—connections to my grandparents, whom I never knew, and their world, which I long to understand.

My passion for collecting clothing prompted friends and relatives to begin handing down their own pieces to me, along with stories of each garment's past—such as a horsehair ball gown by the Fontana Sisters of Rome that had belonged to Ava Gardner and been worn by her to the Oscars, and embroidered bedroom slippers custom made for Jean Howard, a former Ziegfeld Girl and Goldwyn Girl.

My obsession with burlesque began at the age of eighteen when I found two twentieth-century burlesque costumes in a stall cluttered with bric-a-brac at the Twenty-sixth Street flea market in New York. I was drawn to a scrap of shimmering fabric on a wire hanger. Closer examination revealed an old costume composed of a leotard in hot pink lace with nude net inserts, lined with rhinestone piping and black fishnet stockings attached at the bottom. It was thickly woven and much sturdier than any other garment I had seen. Another costume hung beside it: a black jet beaded number on black lace overlay with a flesh-colored corset underneath. Inspecting the inside of these pieces, I detected the great care and attention of the maker; they were lovingly hand-stitched, darned and darned again, as if they had been worn one performance after another.

I surmised that a stripper had once worn these costumes in the early 1950s. They were less revealing than one would imagine, so distant from the contemporary wardrobe (or lack thereof) of topless dancers in de rigueur G-strings and silicone breasts. I had to have these costumes. Clutching my treasured purchases in a flimsy plastic bag, I left the flea market wondering who wore them. *What did she look like? Was she my age?* At home behind closed doors, I tried on these relics of the past and was somehow not surprised at their perfect fit. Whoever their previous owner was, I felt an immediate connection with her.

My new acquisitions led me to begin a self-portrait series in which I wore my costumes, emulating poses of 1940s burlesque queens in their vintage glamour portraits. Attempting to embody my idea of a burlesque queen, I added a black Louise Brooks bob wig, applied red lipstick and heavy black eyeliner, and thought my transformation complete. I denied any aspect of sexuality in my photographs. I was not feigning innocence; I was simply re-creating flat illusions—removed and distant like the archival photos of burlesque queens that I had been collecting.

Looking at old black-and-white prints of Lili St. Cyr, Gypsy Rose Lee, and Ann Corio, I saw women who radiated self-confident sex appeal and appeared to be in complete control of their posturing as they reclined on chaise longues or draped themselves against velvet stage curtains and teased the camera with come-hither eyes. Wearing costumes of exquisite textures and handiwork, the women in these images created an impression of glamour and beauty that greatly inspired me the moment I first laid eyes on them. The original burlesque queens possessed class, skill, and attitude. They were performers and artists.

Like many of my female peers, I was raised in the wake of women's lib, schooled to be independent and to downplay my sexuality in order

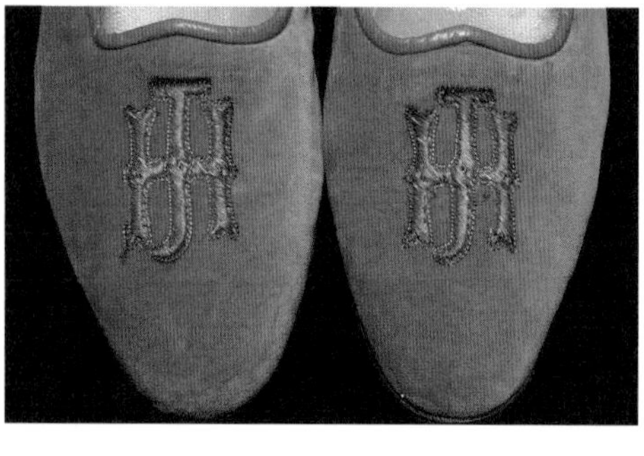

TOP:
Frances Howard, author's grandmother, poses wearing Jean Patou, circa 1920s.

BOTTOM:
Embroidered bedroom slippers belonging to Jean Howard. (Author's collection)

Author's self-portrait series in black jet beaded burlesque costume, 1997.

Author's self-portrait series in pink burlesque costume, 1997.

Author poses in burlesque queen Betty Rowland's costume.

RIGHT:
Betty Rowland in the 1940s wearing the same costume with its additional ostrich feather adornments. The photo was taken backstage with Mimi Reed.

to be taken seriously. In our postfeminist society, many women question whether we really have to choose one role at the expense of the other. In the early twentieth century, women went to burlesque shows to discover the trade secrets of the stripteasers; and now, almost a century later, there lingers for many women a strong attraction to the burlesque queen persona of self-aware sexuality.

I was curious why and when the burlesque queen ceased to exist. I searched for more information about the period of burlesque's demise (late 1950s), but it did not appear to be well documented. There was a big gap between the last generation of queens and the topless dancers currently headlining at strip clubs across the country. I hoped some of the burlesquers were still around to fill in the missing pieces with tales of their glory days. Wanting to absorb the tricks of their trade, I sought out the original owners of my costumes with hopes of learning more about their lost art.

As I began to research burlesque, I continued to collect burlesque costumes from the period between 1900 and 1960 from flea markets, auctions, estate sales, and former burlesque queens selling off their wares. I ended up amassing a large collection, which proved to be a

Pandora's box. Always noting the provenance of a costume when I acquired it, I strung together the names of the women who originally wore them in the 1950s. Soon I started a letter-writing campaign and found myself with a considerable number of pen pals, both long-retired strippers and the aging comedians who had worked with them. At first, some were suspicious and needed coaxing before they would share any personal information. Many had left their careers in burlesque long behind them and wished to forget; others were excited at the chance to pass down their stories.

Through ten years of letters, visits, interviews, and striptease lessons, I have formed close relationships with the last generation of burlesque queens. As I became part of this community, I was initially surprised at how little many of them valued their own place in history. In fact, it became evident that to this older generation of women, "burlesque" was a dirty word in many social circles and not something to be advertised. Historical neglect left me with a sense of injustice on behalf of my burlesque friends. I longed to secure their legacy and put them on a much-deserved pedestal.

I see burlesque queens as artists and their costumes as examples of great craftsmanship. I want to showcase their glory years in this book so that their role in entertainment history can be reexamined and "legitimized." Thus I have compiled a selection of artwork and stories of some of the personalities I have met along the way—inhabitants of a quickly disappearing subculture and art form. This book draws from the treasure trove of archival materials I have collected from those who cared enough to save their memories for a new generation.

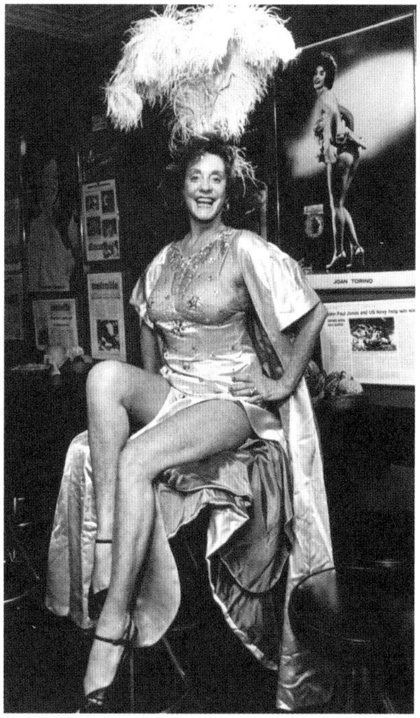

TOP:
Author poses in one of Joan Torino's burlesque costumes designed by Rex Huntington.

BOTTOM:
Joan Torino in the same costume in the 1980s.

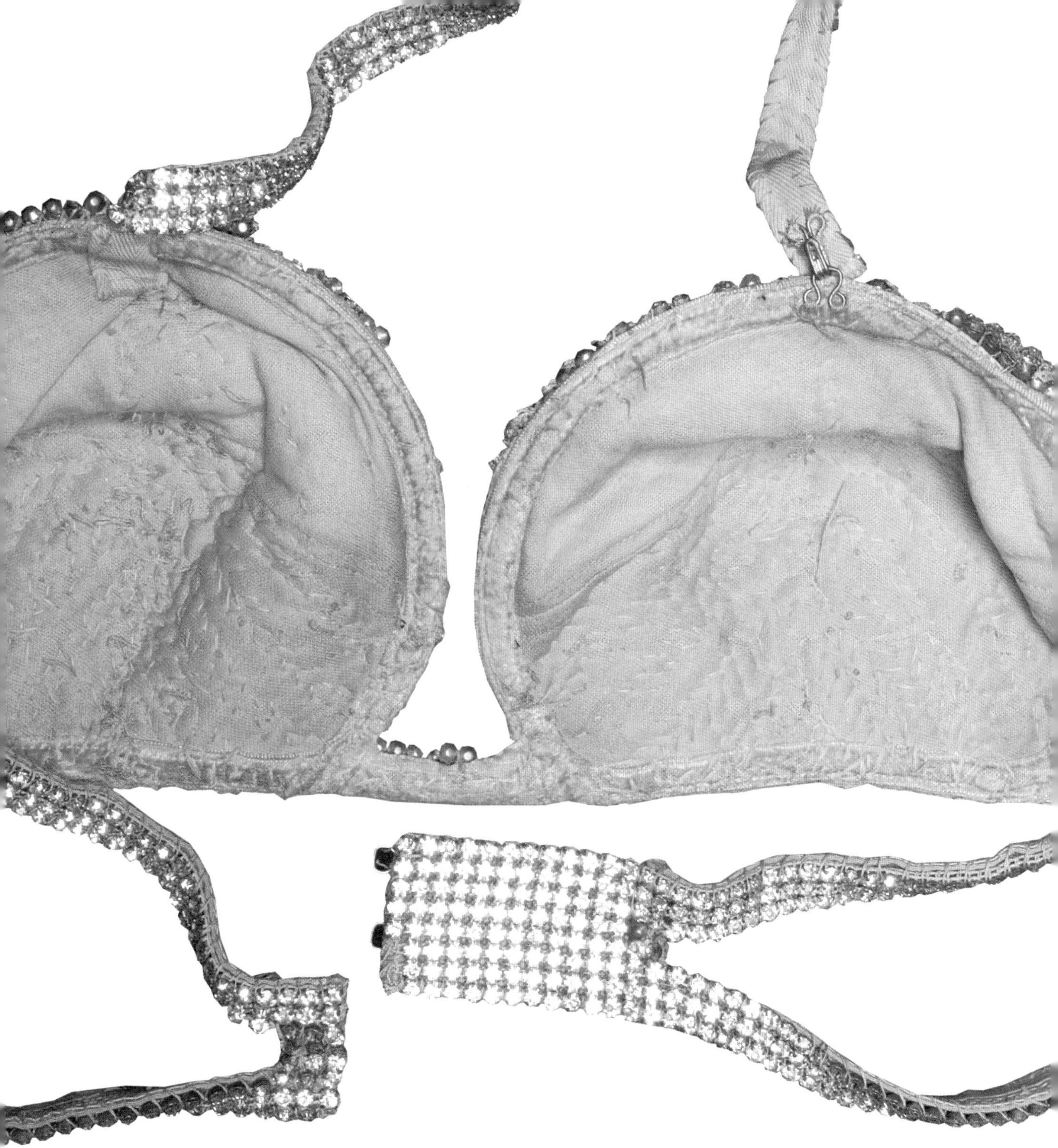

Detail of interior stitching on a rhinestone burlesque outer bra, circa 1940. (Author's collection)

OPPOSITE PAGE:
Large hooks, eyes, and snaps facilitated easy removal of this costume belonging to burlesque queen Betty Rowland.

FOLIES-BERGÈRE
PARIS
602
MARIETTE BERNARDIN
CL. LIÉBERT

INTRODUCTION

The Latin root for "burlesque" comes from *burlare:* to laugh, to make fun of. Early examples of burlesque can be traced to Greek satirical comedies and tragedies, which lampooned contemporary morals and introduced risqué themes into theater. In the fifth century B.C., playwright and poet Aristophanes used parody as an instrument for art and reform. *Lysistrata,* a play he wrote in 411 B.C., is generally considered the first written example of burlesque. In the play, the women of Athens, led by Lysistrata, try to force the men of the city to stop fighting the Peloponnesian Wars by refusing them "sexual favors."

Shakespearean comedies can also be considered burlesque for their fusion of high and lowbrow humor, mocking social mores and class structure. Using slang to reference the comedy of the working class, William Shakespeare just as easily adopted an upper-class lexicon for characters who appealed to his wealthy patrons. In 1600, England's first performance to be labeled burlesque, *The Most Lamentable Comedy & Most Cruel Death of Pyramus* by George Villiers, was a satire of Shakespeare's *A Midsummer Night's Dream*.

In America, burlesque is best known as a form of entertainment that was popular in the first half of the twentieth century and later died with the advent of television and mass communication. American burlesque gained momentum in the late 1800s, when the cities were flooded with immigrants who lacked a common language or form of communal entertainment. The existing American theatrical experience was geared toward the intellectual upper crust, as plays were performed in Anglo-English. Thus, burlesque was born as an alternative to the theater of the bourgeoisie—a true working class form of entertainment whose subject matter was of a universal nature—physical satire, jokes about the body, and a tinge of sex.

The American burlesque queens first captured my interest and

This Folies-Bergère dancer achieved her hourglass figure and wasp waist through a tightly bound corset.

admiration because their particular disregard for social protocol seemed rebellious in an era when women had few career choices. While collecting their biographies, I discovered numerous examples of their forbearers: early Parisian burlesque queens from La Belle Époque.

La Belle Époque, 1871 to 1914, the period of decadent splendor between the liberation of France from the monarchy and the start of World War I, was also known as the "age of women." These decades were marked by true adoration of the female form and all its charms. Art nouveau was the mode of the day, and artists depicted nymphs, sirens, and goddesses in paintings and sculpture. Oscar Wilde and Aubrey Beardsley's renderings of Salome made her an icon of art nouveau sensuality, and started the spread of "Salomania." Oscar Wilde's 1893 play *Salome*, in which the heroine first performs the "dance of the seven veils," opened to success and scandal, as actresses of the day vied for the title role in numerous copycat productions.

The ultimate icon for the femme fatale of La Belle Époque was the courtesan, and several of the great courtesans of this period sought further fame and "legitimacy" on the stage. Many of them enjoyed dual careers as performers at the Folies-Bergère, with dancing acts carefully choreographed to highlight their special "talents" or attributes, such as the legs, which were especially appealing to audiences. The invention of tights in 1798 made the legs all the more visible and marked an important development in the history of burlesque costume and performance costume in general. A man who worked as the hosier for the Paris Opera, later known as Maillot, constructed a very fine, flesh-colored, mesh knit garment that clung to the body. "Tights" were born, and soon the tutu was, too—both subject to intense outrage and protests, similar to the rally cries against the bikini of the mid-twentieth century, which is now a mainstay of swim culture.

Opened in 1869, the Folies-Bergère was the first "legitimate" music hall in Paris. Seats normally cost three francs, shows ran nightly at eight o'clock, and acts included ballet, trapeze, circus performers, singers, one-acts, and operettas. Vaudeville shows also played at the Folies in the 1870s. The content of the entertainment was never too highbrow or literary, as jokes had to be easily comprehensible to the audience and geared to its moral taste. One of the most popular acts at the time was the notorious "Le Pétomane" (the farter), famous for his, ahem, "musical" abilities. His vulgar brand of body/bawdy humor is trademark burlesque comedy. The Folies was also known for the charm of its barmaids, as depicted in Manet's painting, "Bar at the Folies-Bergère" (1881–82), and renowned for its unusual "promenade"—an open-air gallery traversed by ladies of the night seeking a gentleman's favor.

Theater owners exploited the drawing power of beautiful women, particularly that of the courtesans who took to the stage and brought with them a ready following of aristocracy and workmen alike. The public was transfixed with the private lives of these ladies, who were known offstage for their lavish and eccentric costumes as well as for their affairs in the bedchambers of the crowned heads of Europe. Notable mention must be given to the top four contenders (and often rivals) for public attention: Liane de Pougy, La Belle Otero, Emilienne d'Alençon, and Cléo de Mérode.

Liane de Pougy kept a lifelong diary, from which excerpts were published posthumously as *My Blue Notebooks*. In her journals she recorded her days as a star, including details about her wardrobe (often made by couturier Paul Poiret, the first to make pants for women, in the form of his "harem" style trousers), her jewels, gifts from admirers, and her lovers. Though she lived as a temptress, Liane ended up joining a convent before her death in order to atone for her sins.

For sport, the public kept track of the rivalry between Liane and La Belle Otero, (a.k.a. Caroline Otero), a flamboyant Spanish dancer who earned more riches than any of her contemporaries but lost them all to her favorite pastime: gambling. According to one oft repeated tale of Liane and La Belle's feuding, each woman kept tally of who had the most jewels. As an affront to La Belle, Liane went to the opera in a beautiful black velvet gown but with her neck bare, followed by her maidservant, who carried a plush pillow laden with mounds of diamonds, emeralds, rubies, and pearls. In comparison, wearing rings on each finger, diamonds round her neck and wrists, and diadems dripping from her brow, La Belle looked positively vulgar.

Emilienne d'Alençon first appeared in 1889 in a circus act in which rabbits dyed pastel colors wore paper ruffs around their necks. Wearing a tight-fitting ringmaster costume and cracking a whip, she made the rabbits jump through hoops. It is said that she possessed a corset made entirely of diamonds crafted for her by Cartier, perhaps given to her by her lover, Leopold II of Belgium.

Cléo de Mérode, a prima ballerina, was initially shocked to be approached by the owner of the Folies. In her memoirs she writes of her surprise at being asked to perform an "exotic number in his music hall." She then caused great outrage when she posed for a nude sculpture by Jean-Alexandre-Joseph Falguière, the scandal of *tout Paris* when it was exhibited.

What survives of these women's stories is largely hearsay, but it is the stuff of legend. Their onstage acts were tame by comparison to their offstage behavior; they cultivated their routines from classical dance and added their own flavor. Wearing low-cut bustiers and long gowns with carefully placed diamonds to accentuate their cleavage, they were dressed to thrill but never to disrobe. Their figures were voluptuous, and they played up their best assets with their costumes: tights or delicate shoes to show a peek of ankle; belly-baring, diamond-encrusted corsets; multistrand pearl chokers wound tightly around their necks.

Women squeezed into whalebone corsets to achieve the hourglass mode of the day—a "wasp waist" with heaving bosom and round derrière—but the strict fashion edicts of these contraptions made it impossible for female performers to sit down comfortably. Many women rejected roles that did not keep them on their feet and the corset itself was the subject of much music hall satire.

Pretty dancing girls were a staple of Montmartre café society, known for its "artistic" dance and drinking halls. One dancing girl, known as "Nini-la-Belle-en-Cuisse" (Nini of the beautiful thighs), performed at La Reine Blanche. Attempting to present a somewhat more upscale version of these halls, the Moulin Rouge opened in autumn 1889, also in Montmartre. Artist Toulouse-Lautrec's sketches and posters have immortalized the stars of this dance hall—Louise Weber, known as La Goulue, and her partner Valentin; Jane Avril; Yvette Guilbert; Cissie Loftus; May Belfort; and Chocolat, to name a few. In contrast to the lifestyles of Otero and Liane, the Moulin Rouge girls were positively bohemian and did not enjoy the same level of financial success as their counterparts. As dancers and singers who performed in the midst of drunken revelry, these girls had more contact with their audience, without the safety of a full-size stage (theirs was tiny) or the "legitimacy" of the Folies theater.

The showgirls of the Moulin Rouge were known for their trademark cancan, also known as the quadrille, in which dancers would hold one leg outstretched as they jumped on the other leg in time to the music, finally ending in splits on the floor. This required great skill and flexibility to execute gracefully. The girls wore white bloomers and black stockings, which ended mid-thigh and were held up with garters often made from ribbon. Nothing was worn under the bloomers, which were made from calico or cotton and were so thin that often a dark patch was visible in the crotch as the dancers did their high kicks. The creamy expanse of flesh between the end of the bloomers and the beginning of the stockings was the most skin that anyone dared to bare at the time.

La Belle Otero, one of the brightest stars of the Folies-Bergère.

Bloomers were worn by all women during La Belle Époque, with either the backside open (for ventilation) or closed, although only very young girls were known to wear their bloomers sewn shut and it was considered a sign of primness or "good breeding" if a young adult wore her undergarments in this fashion. The subject was ripe for satire, and Yvette Guilbert sang a chanson about it. Known for her wardrobe, Yvette wore her trademark long black gloves onstage every night even though it was the mode for singers of this period to wear white gloves. (Her sartorial choice was said to be dictated by her desire to save on laundry!) Yvette was slim with beautiful long legs, and her costumes were designed accordingly to showcase them. She, along with Jane Avril and Liane de Pougy—all svelte women in a time of fashionably solid female form—started a trend for diet pills. While some women emulated their physique, others subscribed to a regimen of pills to make their breasts larger, perhaps to look more like Otero and Emilienne.

At the Moulin Rouge, all the girls wore their bloomers slit up the front and back along with the traditional black stockings required by management. La Goulue ("the Glutton") had a red heart embroidered on the seat of her bloomers—an early precursor of the stripteaser's "gimmick." La Goulue earned her nickname due to her propensity for drink and was always one to provoke. Quick to pose for her artist and photographer friends au naturel, La Goulue appears in one photo from that time wearing a demi-cup corset, with her breasts bared and nipples visible. Offstage, she was known to have been more interested in women, and it is rumored that she had a torrid affair with another dancer known as La Môme Fromage ("the Cheese Kid").

Artists and writers, icons of the intellectual and artistic avant-garde, frequented the Moulin Rouge and the Folies-Bergère and

TYPES OF THE STAGE
TIGER
2 OZ. FINE CUT
CHEWING TOBACCO.
P. LORILLARD CO.
JERSEY CITY, N.J.
CLEOPATRA.

TYPES OF THE STAGE
TIGER
2 OZ. FINE CUT
CHEWING TOBACCO.
P. LORILLARD CO.
JERSEY CITY, N.J.
SPANISH DANCER.

TYPES OF THE STAGE
PAGE (Female)

TYPES OF THE STAGE
TIGER
2 OZ. FINE CUT
CHEWING TOBACCO.
P. LORILLARD CO.
JERSEY CITY, N.J.
BALLET GIRL.

found the female stars at both venues to be a rich source of inspiration. Jane Avril traveled in literary circles, and Toulouse-Lautrec made his name painting backstage scenes showing cancan dancers in various stages of dress and undress at the Moulin Rouge. The female figure was being celebrated in the arts, from the cold classical forms of statuettes to the warm dancing bodies onstage at the Folies and the Moulin Rouge. Although they predated burlesque queens, these brazen broads clearly paved the way for future generations of "peelers."

One can trace the origins of the striptease as far back as the biblical story of Salome, but one of the first stripteases to be performed onstage was "Le Coucher d'Yvette" during La Belle Époque. Performed in a side alley music hall in Montmartre, this "scene" showed Yvette getting ready for bed. She slowly removed her robe du soir, unlaced her corset ribbons with the help of a *femme de chambre*, unrolled her stockings one by one, and ended up clad only in her bloomers and nightshirt. The act of disrobing and the allure of what remained to be seen (easily conjured in the audience's imagination) were nothing short of thrilling. The response was overwhelming and striptease soon became the latest fad.

"Le Bain de Maid" (The Maid's Bath) and "Suzanne et la Grande Chaleur" (Suzanne in the Heat Wave) were just two of the new "scenes" that sprang up. The premise, of course, was for the young woman to remove her clothing in a variety of scenarios. Similar to today's movie fantasy sequences, these early pantomimes provided the audience with a treat soon to be relegated to peep show booths. (The woman never got completely nude during these scenes, as it was only 1894.)

Though nudes were popularized in art at this time, they only appeared in painting salons if the canvas adhered to strict guidelines—the rendering of a nude figure had to be "classical or historical in pretext." In late 1894 France got its first taste of onstage "nudity" due to the current vogue for *tableaux vivants* (living pictures), which were very much the rage of the Académie Française and translated well onto the stage. Although the public had become used to seeing partial nudity and tights showcasing female curves, it was still considered naughty and marked only a small step toward the first "nudes" onstage.

Actors wearing skin-colored unitards presented scenes on stage. These "nude" performers had to remain motionless—as still as statues—for fear of offending the audience, or worse, public officials. Dramatic renderings of biblical scenes became commonplace, as each

OPPOSITE PAGE:
Cigarette cards depict popular female burlesque "Types of the Stage."

OPPOSITE PAGE:
A lady of the stage, 1916.

venue vied to outdo the other with increasingly daring female nude spectacles. The Folies-Bergère took this idea one step further and began presenting scenes of nudes incorporated into the background scenery—even suspending them from the chandeliers—all in the name of performance art.

Theater and music hall owners printed postcards and posters featuring the star attractions in order to entice customers as well as men passing by on the street to attend shows. Chewing tobacco advertisements in which "ballet queens" or Folies and music hall ladies posed as "models" also helped to spread the performers' fame. Sold at newsstands, penny postcards bore images of these beautiful women—the more flimsy the attire, the better. One of the first advertisements for the Moulin Rouge featured Jane Avril, as rendered by Toulouse-Lautrec himself. Cigarette packs also carried small, pocket-sized images of Otero and her peers, early "pinup" queens culled from the stage.

As Parisian nightlife flourished, so too did English music halls with their version of dancing girls. In the late 1860s, John Hollingshead, founder of the Gaiety Theater in London, created his own model of chorus girl: the Gaiety Girl. American burlesque started with the influx of European producers bringing shows across the Atlantic to premiere in New York. America's immigrant communities undoubtedly influenced the producers of *The Black Crook* in 1866. Staged in an established uptown theater, it introduced the Parisian cancan to middle-class audiences in New York.

In 1868, the English troupe known as The British Blondes (thus named for their peroxide-yellow hair) led by Lydia Thompson came to New York in a production entitled *Ixion*. Lydia and her troupe of chorus girls are credited with shifting the emphasis of burlesque performance from comic sketches to displays of overt female sexuality. *Ixion*'s particular novelty was that it showcased its chorus girls and lady principals in tights that revealed their feminine curves, which caused much scandal. For the first time in America, one could see a woman's leg, her anatomy, her form in a public performance. An exposed ankle was considered shocking at the time, so one can only imagine the furor the British Blondes caused with their scanty attire.

The drama of disrobing became an actual fad in the United States in the late nineteenth century when a dancer known as Little Egypt introduced her version of the belly dance—called "the hooch dance"—

GIRLIE GIRLS

in 1893. Her costume was inspired by Eastern dress: a bolero jacket, a chemise, a sash and harem pantalettes.

For all the uproar over the nearly naked women in burlesque around the turn of the century, burlesque shows remained largely satires of popular theater and focused primarily on the dialogue and comics. With few exceptions, women generally appeared in the chorus or in bit parts. They were often called "beefstock" for their heavy build, a fashionable by-product of the decadent lifestyle of the period.

"Sister acts" had been a constant in music halls for some time. The Barrison Sisters, who appeared in the 1890s, were among the first to exploit the idea of a perfectly formed troupe of female "siblings" performing song and dance numbers in unison. In fact, Lona Barrison and her "sisters" Sophia, Inger, Olga, and Gertrude, were not related at all, though they could pass with their similar build, identical makeup, and blonde wigs. Offsetting their innocent appearance, a cigarette dangled permanently from their lips during their numbers, as well as in their publicity material. Surely their reputation as provocative, limber ladies helped grow their fan base. In one act, the Barrison Sisters raised their skirts as they danced, teasing the audience with the taunt, "Would you like to see my pussy?" As they lifted their skirts above their waists, each girl revealed her handmade underwear—which had a live kitten attached to her crotch! The Barrison Sisters walked an extremely fine line between eroticism and vulgarity.

The Barrison Sisters.

OPPOSITE PAGE:
A line of chorus girls, circa 1920.

Until the early 1920s, American burlesque remained focused on the comics and was very similar to vaudeville in its format. Gradually, with the explosion of Broadway and the need for a less intellectual form of entertainment, burlesque became the "poor man's theater." In contrast, impresario Florenz Ziegfeld's Follies were known as "rich man's burlesque"—beautiful showgirls in expensive clothes and jewels, elaborate lighting and sets, delivering cleaned-up jokes from cleaned-up comics.

Beginning in 1907 in New York City, Ziegfeld made near-nudity respectable in the legitimate theater and at his rooftop nightclub. In these venues, elaborately costumed chorus girls known as "Ziegfeld Girls" paraded through opulent stage sets wearing sensational and revealing costumes. Their elaborate chorine costumes emphasized and

OPPOSITE PAGE:
Examples of Beefstock Girls, circa 1930.

exposed their femininity, hinting at nudity yet never truly revealing it. Ziegfeld mastered early burlesque methods of seducing an audience, such as silhouetted nudes and still *mise-en-scènes* of his scantily clad chorus girls. He spared no expense on production designer Ben Ali Haggin's *tableaux vivants*, in which women posed as living statuary, often arranged to depict famous works of art—thus making their near-nudity "acceptable."

The Dolly Sisters were just one example of Ziegfeld's star attractions. Unlike the aforementioned sister acts, the Dollys were actual twins from Hungary. The sisters first made a name for themselves onstage in vaudeville, and then in the Ziegfeld Follies of 1911. They quickly became stars, racking up millionaire admirers and collections of jewels. Icons of the flapper age, their short hair and painted Cupid's bow lips inspired trends when they hit the other side of the Atlantic for the first time. Accustomed to the wardrobe finery of a Ziegfeld production (he dressed them in diamond bodices and headdresses, with skirts of white ostrich) they gained a reputation for walking out of shows if they weren't pleased with their costuming and salaries. They were international stars and role models for countless sister acts that followed in their wake.

By the early 1920s, in order to compete with the Follies, vaudeville, and "legitimate" theater, burlesque producers made their chorus girls more of a focus—having them wear less and less and shining the spotlight on them more and more, until striptease was born as a popular phenomenon. A full orchestra opened the show, followed by a comic act, and then the burlesque stripper. Just as men today might claim to read *Playboy* for the articles, men of that era would ostensibly go to burlesque shows to see the great comics. Burlesque did have a female audience as well. Women would go with their dates or even families to see a good show, and to inspect the wardrobes of the queens.

However in the 1930s, as public morals groups formed by citizens in reaction to the decadent 1920s grew at an alarming rate, burlesque theater owners were simultaneously pressuring their star acts to reveal more and more flesh through "flashing." Zorita, one of the most outstanding burlesque queens, filled me in further on the practice of flashing (or in her words, "flashing your knish"). She recalled, "There was a red light in the orchestra pit and when the red light was on, it meant the cops were in, so play it safe. When the red light went out, all bets were off. There were times you would work in the theater and you might do two shows and be covered, and the third

Theatrical
CHICAGO

Theatrical
CHICAGO

Strand

1920s chorus girls in their finery attracted audiences.

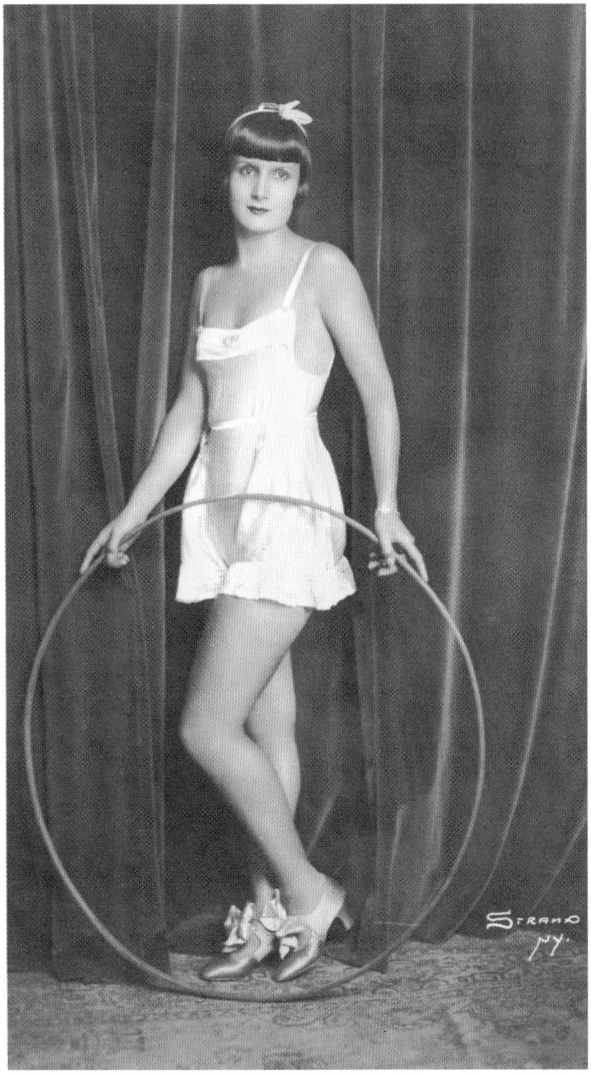

A 1920s chorus girl dressed up to embody the popular male fantasy of an innocent young girl.

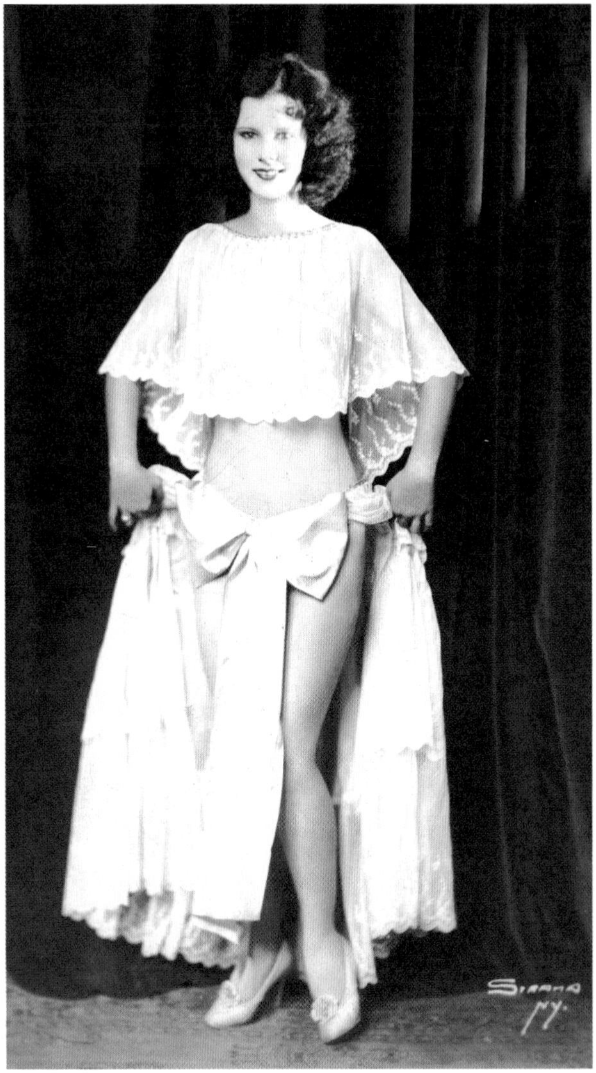

A giant bow reveals and covers her "present."

show the red light was off and so then you flashed. And your customers were so used to that, and they knew that if they saw that you didn't flash, the law was in. And so, they just usually sat over for the second shift or came in later on that week. Some of the customers came in and saw the show two and three times."

In the early 1930s notorious burlesque queen Margie Hart, with her bright red hair, blue eyes, and feisty personality, was often discussed in conjunction with flashing. In fact many burlesque queens hold Margie Hart's flashing responsible for Mayor La Guardia's final shutdown of burlesque in New York City in 1939. According to Zorita, who was friendly with Margie, "I thought she was fun. [She] always had her knish dyed bright red. She flashed knish and maybe gave too long of a flash at the wrong time, when the red light was on."

Sherry Britton, who did not get along with Margie, has a slightly different story: "I don't know how much further you could go than Margie Hart, who was the first one to flash. And she had natural red hair. So you could see it. She had a detective for a boyfriend, and he'd always warn her before the censors came, and she'd cover up. She got another boyfriend and [the detective] got very jealous and didn't warn her the next time, and there she was—she was caught by the censors." Another popular myth purports that Margie performed without a G-string because it ruined the line of her stage wardrobe, possibly contributing to her brush with the law.

Regardless of the exact motivations for his actions, the practice of flashing among burlesque queens surely helped prompt La Guardia to begin his moral campaign of cleaning up the smut in Manhattan. Sherry explains some of the laws that went into effect after La Guardia's initial shutdown:

> The first time [La Guardia shut down burlesque] was 1939 here in New York. There were seventeen burlesque theaters in Manhattan, the Bronx, New York City. He [eventually] permitted them to open again [because] it was Depression time, and closing seventeen theaters would've had a great impact on costume designers, photographers, press agents. Everything associated with those theatres. So we were permitted to open again with some no-no's. And one of them was that you were not allowed to rouge your nipples. This is long before pasties came about. And my nipples were rose-colored,

STRAND

> and under the blue light they turned a very vivid red. Three burly detectives came backstage, handkerchiefs in hand, to make sure that I wasn't rouging my nipples. And I had to stand there—that was the law—while the three of them [checked to see] whether it rubbed off. One would've been enough. No, the three of them.

Restrictive ordinances were enacted and then overturned, until finally, in 1939, burlesque was outlawed permanently in New York City. This marked the beginning of the slow demise of classic burlesque with its full orchestras, productions, and players. The shutdown of the industry affected many people: performers, musicians, theater workers, and the attendant businesses as well—costumers, theater suppliers, photography studios, boarding houses, hotels, and restaurants.

As burlesque production numbers faded out, nightclubs where strippers were the sole focus gained popularity. Though male comics went on to legitimate theater, film, and television, burlesque women and their risqué stripteases were relegated to nightclubs and theaters that got seedier as time passed. These nightclubs sold liquor, which the previous burlesque theaters did not, and there was more pressure from the audience to "work strong"—in other words, to show total nudity. Once widely considered as artists in their own right, many burlesque queens felt they were no longer being treated or respected as performers. The audience wanted nakedness, not artful nudity. They wanted instant gratification, not entertainment.

This book celebrates the last of the great burlesque queens, the twentieth-century women who, through their stage personas, costumes, and choreography, created myths that left a lasting impression on American entertainment.

Burlesque queen Margie Hart is often cited for contributing to the final shutdown of burlesque theaters in New York City.

OPPOSITE PAGE:
Like Salome, Honey Bee Keller drops her veil.

Burlesque Family Tree

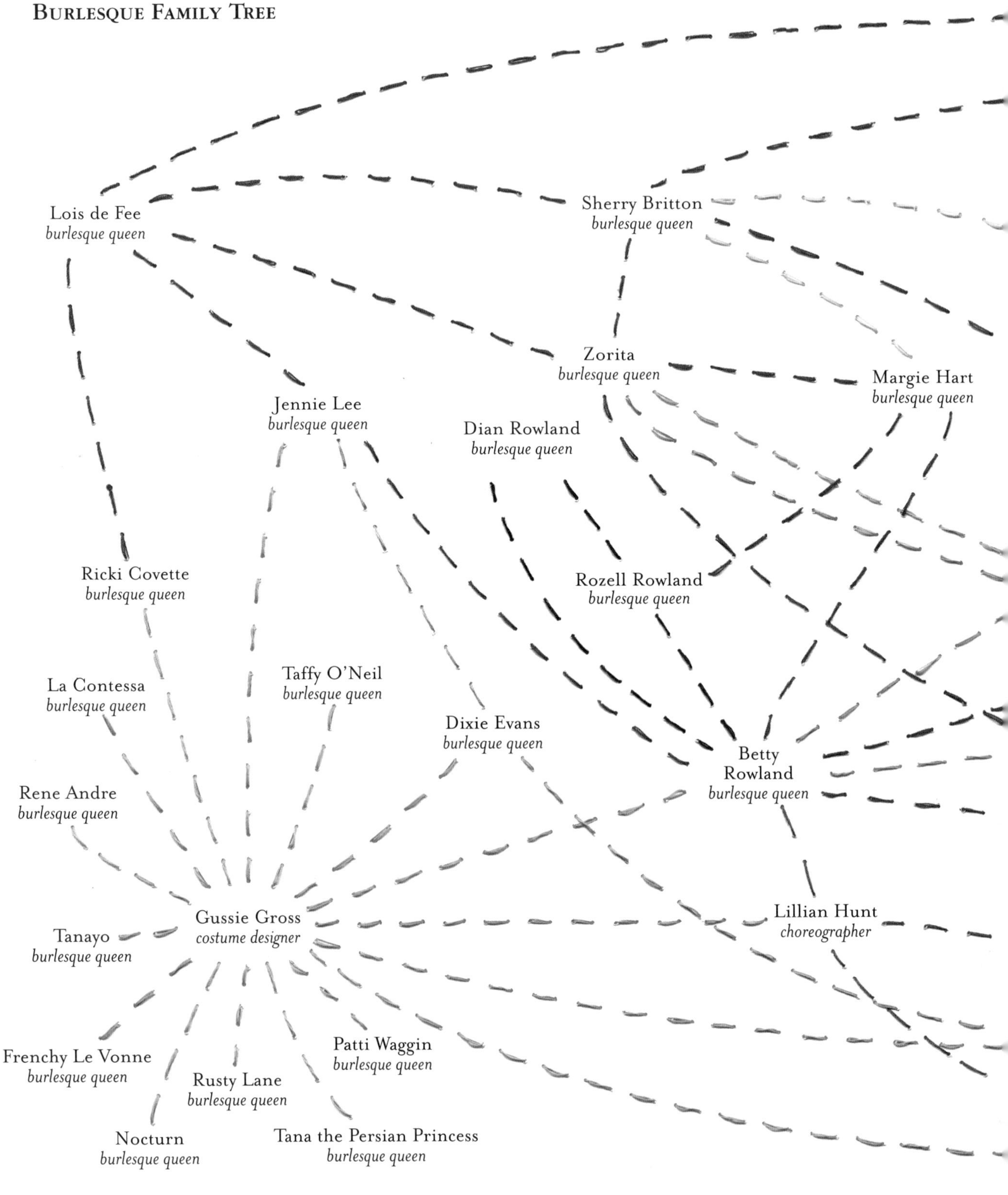

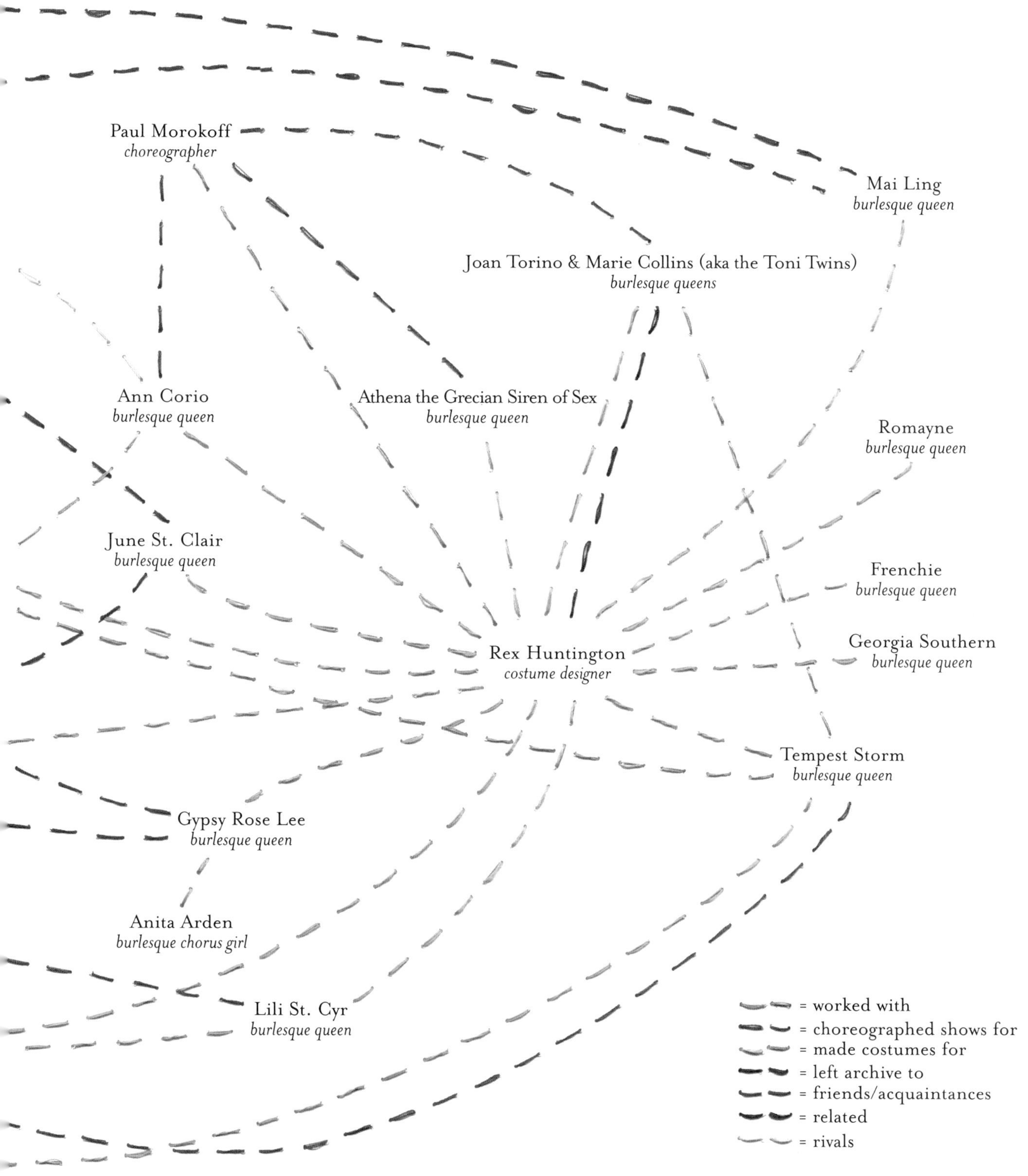

Paul Morokoff
choreographer
Mai Ling
burlesque queen
Joan Torino & Marie Collins (aka the Toni Twins)
burlesque queens
Ann Corio
burlesque queen
Athena the Grecian Siren of Sex
burlesque queen
Romayne
burlesque queen
June St. Clair
burlesque queen
Frenchie
burlesque queen
Rex Huntington
costume designer
Georgia Southern
burlesque queen
Tempest Storm
burlesque queen
Gypsy Rose Lee
burlesque queen
Anita Arden
burlesque chorus girl
Lili St. Cyr
burlesque queen
= worked with
= choreographed shows for
= made costumes for
= left archive to
= friends/acquaintances
= related
= rivals

For the burlesque queen, the single most important contributing factor to her success was an elaborate wardrobe. Headlining stars were meticulously made-up and costumed in order to transform into sex goddesses onstage, where dazzling costumes visually transported the audience to alternate realities. Designers interpreted the optical illusion of nudity through creative use of beadwork, sequins, and netting, often tricking the audience into believing they were seeing more flesh than was actually being exposed. Sally Rand, the burlesque queen world renowned for her "fan dance," used this technique to great effect in her act. While the audience thought that she was completely bare save for the giant ostrich feathers she carried in each hand, she actually wore a flesh-colored bodysuit.

Burlesque queens made their stage entrances in full evening regalia, sometimes replete with headpiece, gloves, and cape. A standard elegant burlesque costume consisted of an outer-piece garment designed to resemble a floor-length gown. Beneath the outer gown were panels, made of strips of embroidered or sequined fabric around the hips, with layers of chiffon or satin fabric hanging down the front and back of the legs to the ankles. Covering the bust was an outer bra which hid yet another layer of net bra, and then pasties. Last but not least was the ever present G-string. The stripper removed each piece, one by one, every layer as extravagant as the last.

Though ostensibly worlds removed from the couture ateliers, the art of fitting a burlesque costume for a performer was similar to that of fitting couture clothing for a model or client. The measurement process alone could take hours. A sample page from burlesque costume designer Rex Huntington's sketchbooks notes a few of the necessary measurements: "waist to crotch-front; waist to anklebone-outside; crotch to anklebone-outside" and so forth. From headdress to gloves,

Comic, circa 1950.

OPPOSITE PAGE:
Gussie Gross measures a stripper backstage at the Los Angeles Follies Theater.

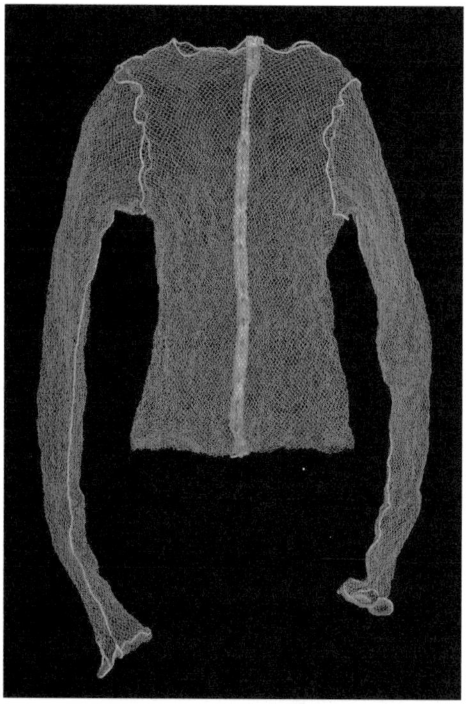

Pink fishnet body stocking top. (Author's collection)

OPPOSITE PAGE (TOP):
Flesh pasties with pink "pearl" nipples by Gussie Gross. (Author's collection)

OPPOSITE PAGE (BOTTOM):
Elaborate outer G-string with accompanying inner G-string belonged to a burlesque dancer known as Chiquita. (Author's collection)

each piece of the costume had to fit its owner perfectly. Once a muslin pattern was made, there could be up to ten fittings before a costume was deemed performance-ready.

Unlike street wear, burlesque costumes needed to be engineered to stay in place. The costumes had to be durable, as they were worn again and again in high-energy routines. Big brass hooks, eyes, and snaps were used to ensure easy access to the garments underneath and extra-heavy-duty zippers assured an easy slide down the back. Velcro did not exist at the time—these girls had to be skilled and graceful to make a complicated contraption look deceptively easy to remove.

Needless to say, with all its layers in a single outfit, well-made burlesque attire was expensive. Performers were required to furnish their own gowns, usually a repertoire of four to five gowns per season on the road. The biggest stars spent $400 to $600 per gown (the equivalent of $2,600 to $3,600 per costume today). Considering that top stars would make anywhere from $800 to $1,800 a week, depending on the city and theater they were performing in, they were spending about half of their monthly salaries on costumes alone.

In small towns and big cities across America, the runways of the burlesque theater were a veritable fashion show for those who didn't have access to Parisian couture or the latest issue of *Vogue* magazine. Many women came to see the queens perform in order to take notes on their attire and translate it into their own wardrobe. The top stars received countless fan letters from women asking them about their wardrobe, where they had costumes made, and tips for a good sex life with their husbands. The average housewife seemed curious about how she could attain a bit of the burlesque queen's sexual allure without the taint of her profession. However often the burlesque queen was slighted by polite society, female fans had an undeniable interest in her life and sexuality.

Betty Rowland, a famed burlesque queen who had many intricate gowns, told me that she once "loaned a girl one of my costumes to have her pictures taken in—professional pictures, to give to her husband for Christmas or for his birthday or some occasion. She had the costume and everything, and went over to Westmores and had her makeup and

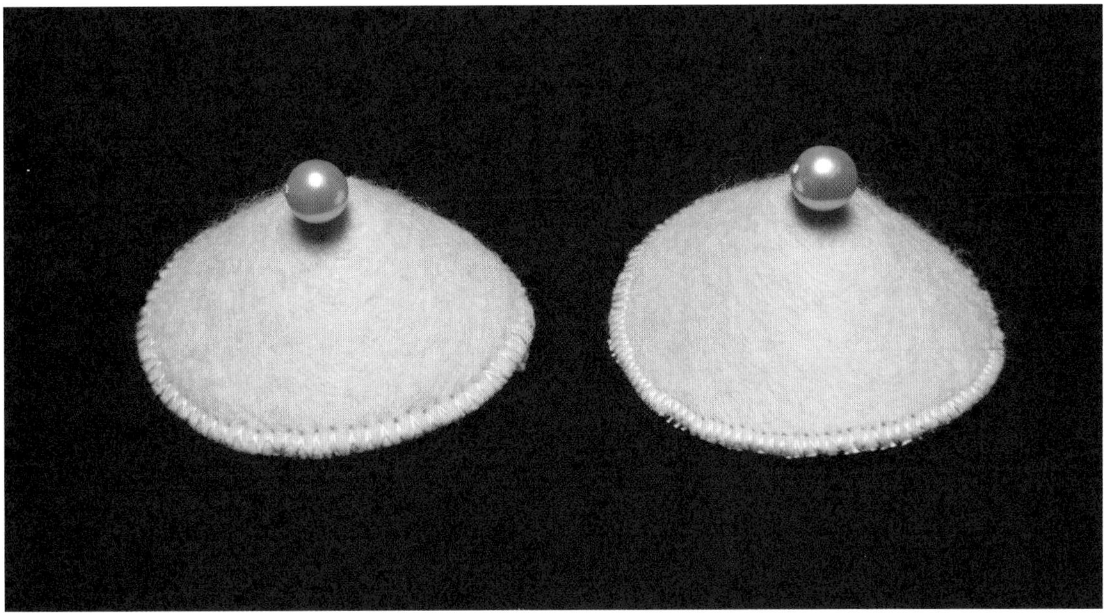

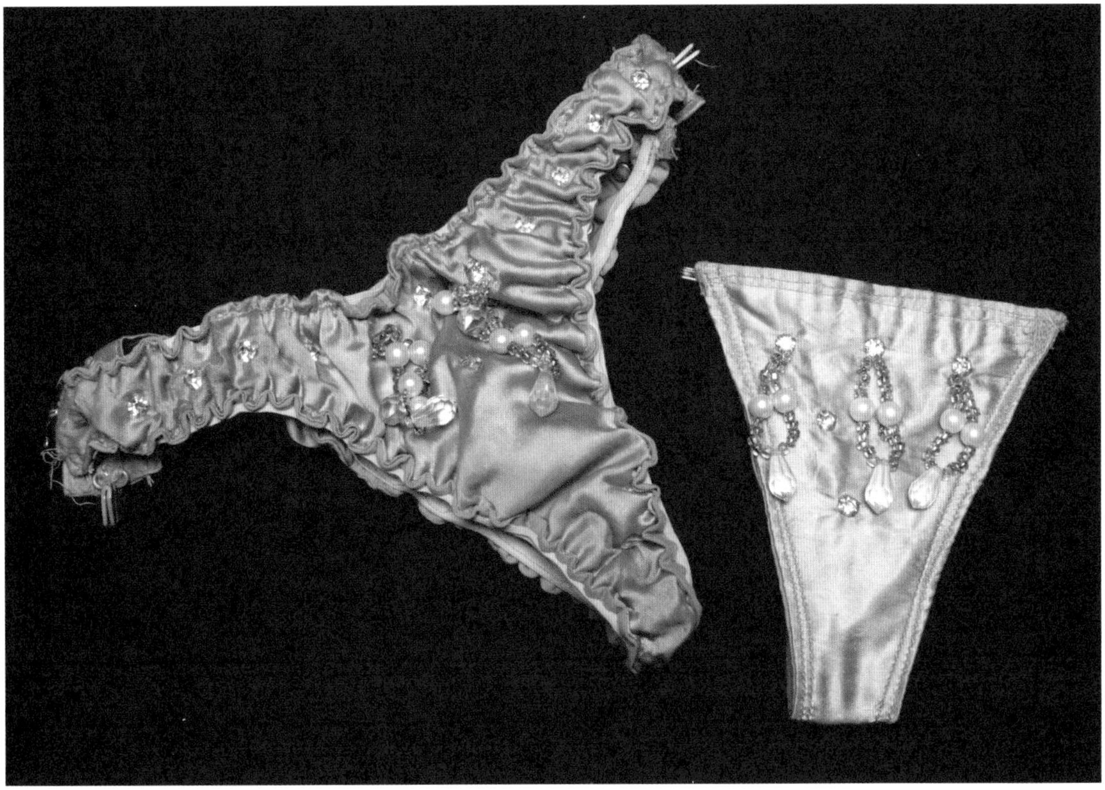

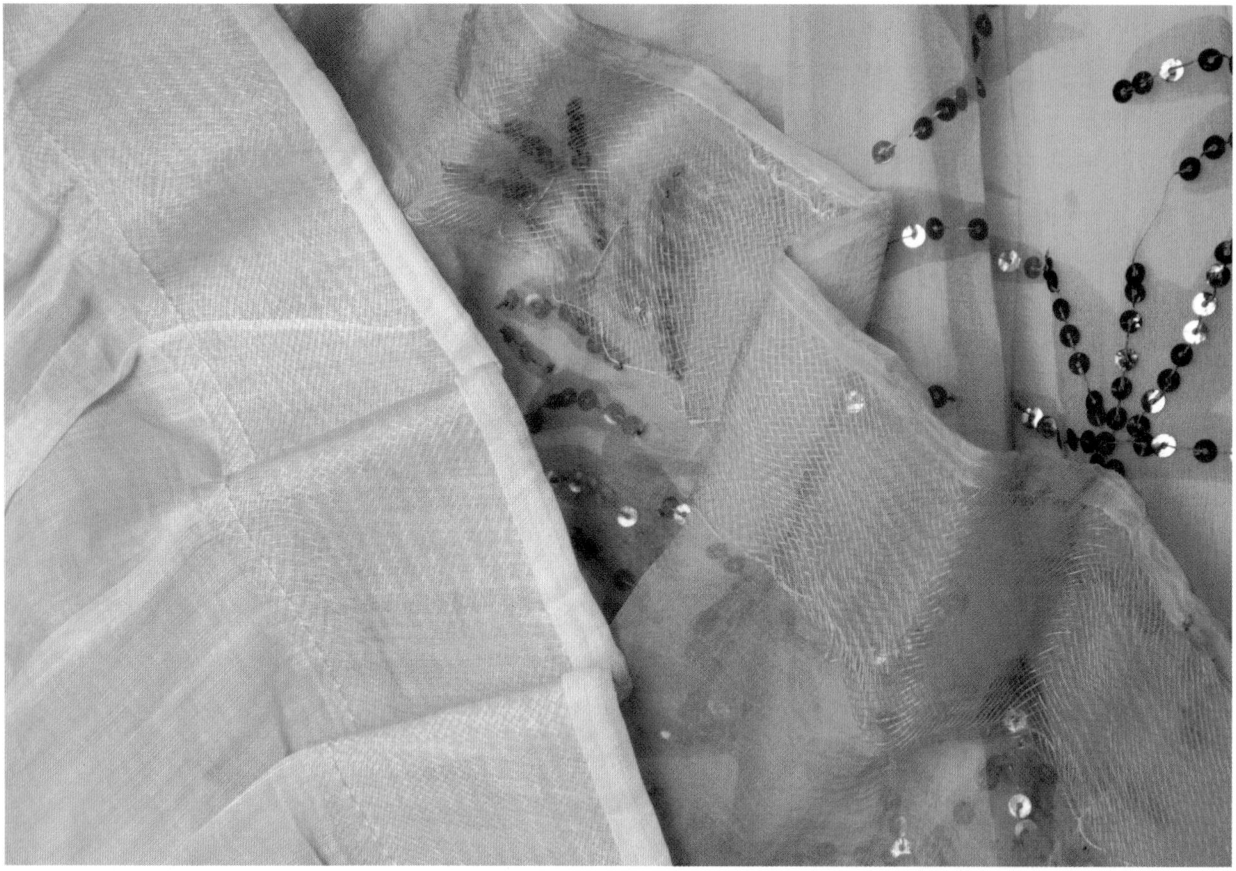

This overskirt belonged to burlesque queen Winnie Garrett. It incorporates horsehair for fullness and shape, and hand-embroidered sequins to enhance the fabric's soft pattern. (Author's collection)

OPPOSITE PAGE:
This handcrafted, elegant, multitiered seed pearl headdress belonged to Sherry Britton. Horsehair and a small comb inside kept it in place while she danced. (Author's collection)

her hair done. And she just looked lovely. And the pictures came out just fine, and her husband was very happy."

Fashion designers consistently mined burlesque costumes for ideas and Hollywood costume designers translated the burlesque looks onto the silver screen. There are many examples in Hollywood films of the use of burlesque costume as a device for representing risqué sexuality. However, celluloid often removed or gentrified burlesque's inherently bold suggestion of sex. In *Lady of Burlesque*, a 1943 film based on Gypsy Rose Lee's novel *G-String Murders*, costume designer Edith Head's gowns for star Barbara Stanwyck managed to maintain a fine balance of sexiness and class, rather than the overt sex appeal of a typical burlesque stripper's wardrobe. An atypical stripper, Gypsy was exquisitely dressed by high society fashion designer Charles James, who used corsetry to grand effect in his work both for Gypsy and his Park Avenue clientele.

Images of scantily attired burlesque queens have been passed down through the ages, paving the way for contemporary costume both to

embody and question current feminine ideals. Madonna's Gaultier-designed cone bra and bustier worn on her "Blond Ambition" tour recall the early witticism of showgirl and striptease style—ingeniously designed and devised costumes that exploited the wearer's best assets and satirized sex appeal in the process.

Hollywood movie stars relied on studio costume designers to make them look their best on screen, whereas burlesque stars had exceptionally collaborative relationships with their costume designers. Each woman worked hard to separate herself from the pack, as a unique costume could win notices in the newspapers and earn the performer a certain status as a "style icon" on the burlesque circuit.

Among the designers who serviced the East Coast burlesque circuit from the 1930s to the 1960s were: Madame Etoile and Mother Haines for gowns; Brooks Costumes, which also made circus costumes; Betty Meyers for G-strings and bras; Billy Livingston, an inhouse designer at the Copa Cabana nightclub who made burlesque costumes as a sideline; and Rex Huntington, who worked with the biggest stars on the East Coast, including Gypsy Rose Lee, Sally Rand, Ann Corio, Zorita, Georgia Southern, Lili St. Cyr, and Tempest Storm.

In Los Angeles, strippers worked with Jack of Hollywood, who had a design studio on La Brea Avenue, and Lili St. Cyr, a famous burlesque queen, had a lingerie shop in West Hollywood. Her designs were based on her own stripper wardrobe and were a big hit with burlesque queens and civilians alike. Indisputably, the most productive West Coast burlesque costume designer in the 1940s and 50s was Gussie Gross who, like Rex Huntington, also counted among her clients Lili St. Cyr, Betty Rowland, and Tempest Storm.

Many of these burlesque costume designers' biographies and archives have been lost to history, as burlesque itself was considered illegitimate and dismissed as a marginal art form. Their work, though often copied and referenced in their own time and even to this today, remains to be investigated and celebrated by costume historians and museums. Fortunately, the archives of two of the most prolific designers of the golden days of burlesque—Rex Huntington and Gussie Gross—survive.

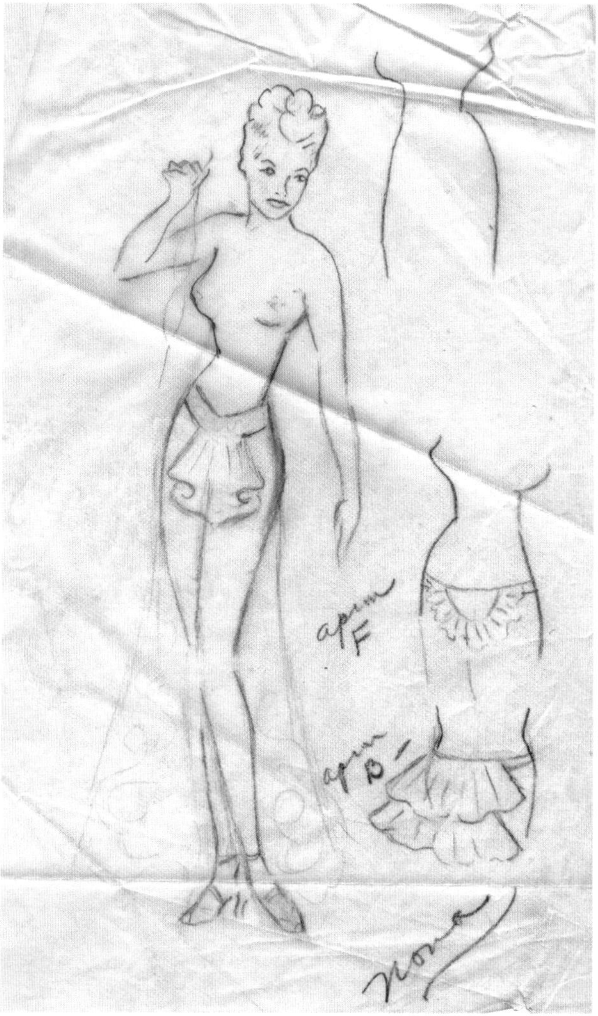

The "sexy housewife," a common male fantasy as sketched by Gussie Gross.

Jean Paul Gaultier's costume for Madonna on her 1990 Blond Ambition tour bears an uncanny resemblance to this sketch by Rex Huntington from the 1960s.

Jane Russell's costume in the RKO motion picture The French Line *(1954), pictured above, is remarkably similar to the 1950s burlesque costume from the author's collection on the right, demonstrating the striking parallels between costuming for the stage and film.*

Rita lost 8 pounds in dance: "It was the toughest dancing job I ever had."

Among the magazine clippings that Gussie Gross saved over the years is an article showing pictures of Rita Hayworth as Salome in a 1953 Columbia motion picture of the same name. Hayworth's costume was designed by Jean Louis. Gussie made variations on the "Salome" harem costume for a number of clients, including Shiva and Tana the Persian Princess, pictured here in Polaroids.

HOLLYWOOD
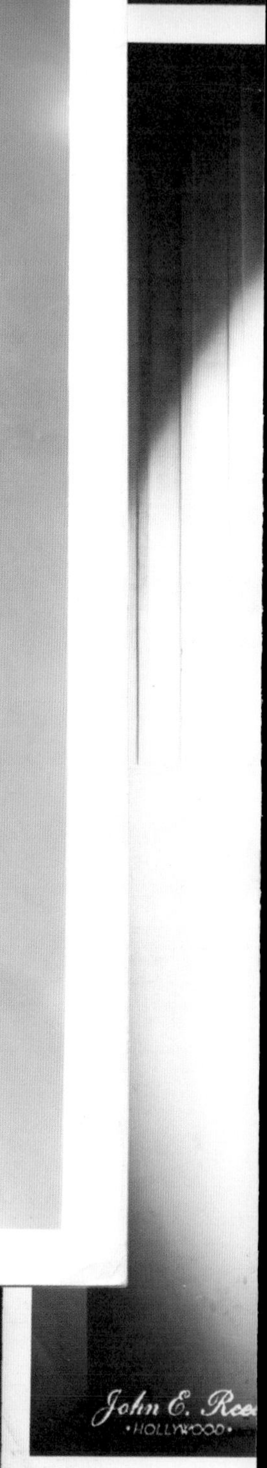
HOLLYWOOD

OPPOSITE PAGE:
Betty Rowland strikes a classic queen pose. Note her expanse of thigh and décolletage.

THIS PAGE:
A housewife friend of Betty Rowland's borrowed the legendary burlesque queen's costume for her own professional photo shoot. Her modesty is evident; she adds a layer of black ruffles and clutches the negligee closed over her breasts.

Betty Rowland says that some housewives would even come to work in burlesque for a spell: "One little gal, she used to work every once in a while because she wanted a new Frigidaire, and her husband had a regular job. So she'd work a few weeks and buy a new refrigerator, and then she'd be gone."

Tempest Storm at Lou Walters' Latin Quarter nightclub in a gown by Rex Huntington. Her inscription reads: "To Rex, The dress caused a sensation. Tempest Storm."

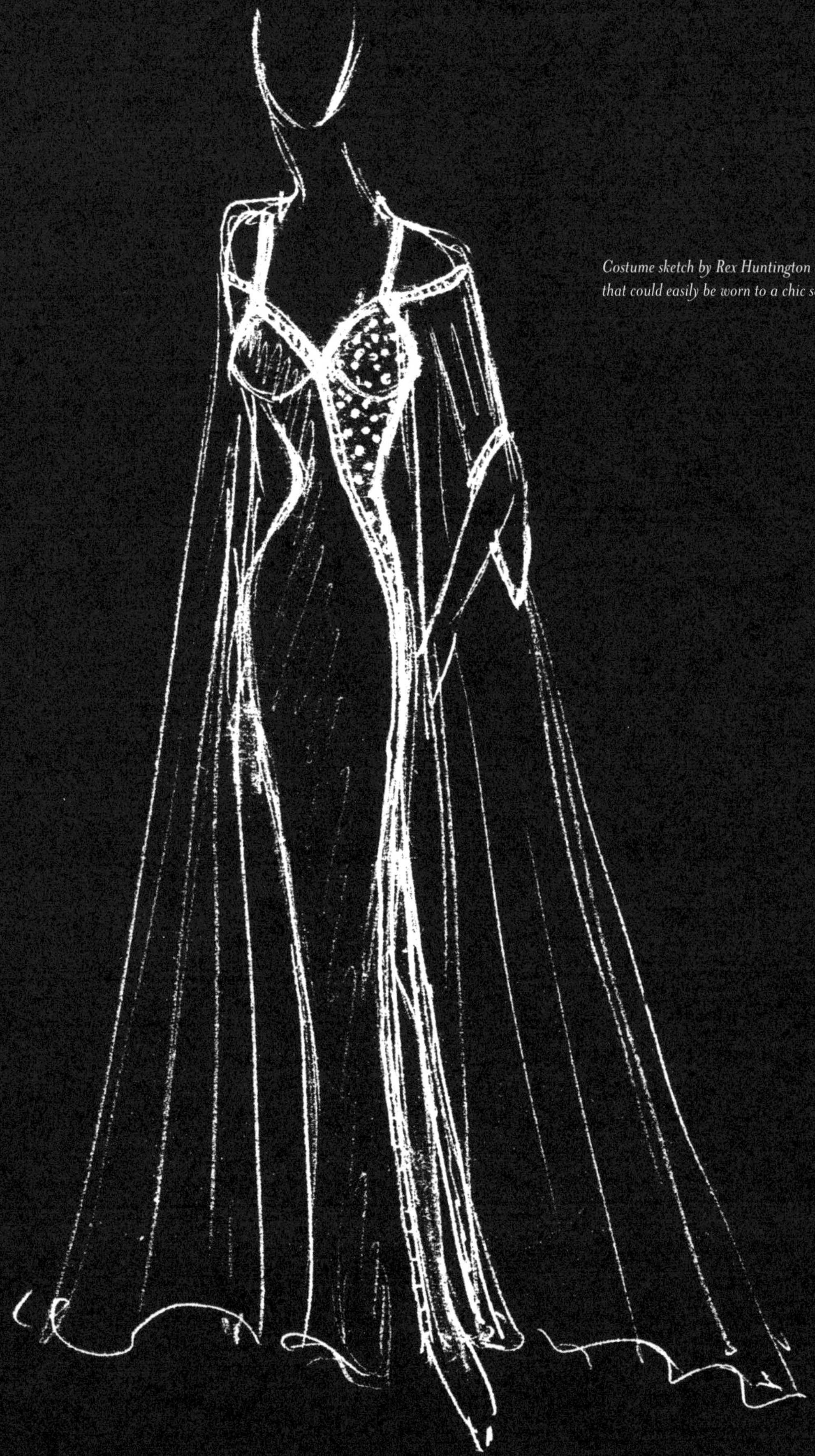

Costume sketch by Rex Huntington of an elegant gown that could easily be worn to a chic society soiree.

The symbiotic relationship between high fashion and costume design is evident when comparing this elegant (and likely expensive) gown to a sketch for a striptease costume by Gussie Gross.

Venus
Use 1 Gross Rh in Bra + apron ruffle
Band 26" fin
19"
36 1/2
6
8
10
zip in gl
24 yard around Bottom

Exotic Lily
Black satin
Corsette of black nylon tulle

3/4 cup solid silver seq.
3 yds seq. each cup

6 ply both sides.
15 yds single strand
7 yds dbl strand

line

OPPOSITE PAGE:
Gussie Gross sketch for Lili St. Cyr.

THIS PAGE:
Lili St. Cyr's lingerie catalogue, "Intimate Secrets."

Another "Intimate Secrets" catalogue featuring a selection of "tantalizing sequined pasties."

FOLLOWING PAGE:
A page from Rex Huntington's costume ledger showing some of the biggest names in burlesque, the gowns they ordered,

July 30	JAN MARVIS –	BLUE sequin gown & CAPE
30	TANA LOUISE	~~Orange~~ Orange sequin gown & coat
Aug 14	ANN CORIO	wardrobe –
Aug – 20	DORIAN DENNIS	SILVER SEQUIN & white gown
21	ZORITA	SEQUIN SUIT
Sept. 1	Tana Louise	red sequin gown, cape gold flowers –
Sept 1	Marelyn Marshall	refringe blue gown –
Sept. – 21	Mattison Trio	2 blk long leotards & repair
Oct – 5	Ann Corio	red sequin powder my Back Costume
Oct – 15	Marie Bradley	wool coat & dress
Oct – 15	Hope Diamond	Prop covers –
Oct – 28	Tempest Storm	Shrimp colored neglige
Nov 3	Suzanne Bernard.	gold jersey & blk & gold gowns
Nov 9	Ann Corio	pants – hat – net – ~~leg~~ – ~~bra~~ pants
Nov 14	Zorita	blue stretch bull fighter outfit –
Nov 15	Tempest Storm	blue neglige & repair & corset
Dec 1	Tempest Storm	shrimp corset – 40.00 repair dress zip – 2.50 Cle…
Dec 10	Peppy Powell	3 gowns Blue – white and peach – Coat cap…
Dec 10	Marion Russell	hot pink sequin
Dec 10	Monica Stevens	redo two gowns –
Dec 10	Monica Stevens	2 panels 2 pr. pants plain 2 – fanc…
Dec 31	Ann Corio	wardrobe
1966		
Jan 11 –	ANN CORIO	net pants
Jan 16 –	ANN Corio	3 Bill Baileys (6) each. Collars & Cuffs 1.50 set Bows & Cuffs
Jan 18	ZORITA	pink sequin gown
Jan 18	ZORITA	4 sequin blouses –
Jan 24	TEMPEST Storm	ORCHID NEG –
Jan 29	Athena	~~Rhinestone~~ Costume (Rhinestone)
Jan 29	Trinka Morgan	Gold & Blk fringe shake costume
Feb 3	Marianne	orchid neglige with feathers
		blk patent pants & vest –

	Cost	Dep.	Bal	
	275.00		275.00	Pd.
	250.00		250.00	Pd.
	22.50			Pd.
	250.00	125.00 100.00	~~125.00~~ 25.00	
	150.00	100.00	50.00	Pd.
	250.00	—	250.00	
	90	55	35.00	Pd.
	75.		75.00	Pd.
	125?			Pd.
	110.00			Pd.
	20.00			Pd.
	75.00			Pd.
	235.00			Pd.
	20.00			Pd.
	150.00	60 –	90	Pd.
	115.00			Pd.
12.00 ~~[illegible]~~ $2.50	57.00	10	47.00	Pd Bal
	450.00	100.	150.00 ~~200.00~~ Pd. 100.00	$100.00
	300.00	100.00		Pd.
	50.00	25.00	25.00	Pd
	$40.00			Pd.
	$182.50			Pd
	$2.50			
	24.50			Pd.
	$175.00	50	$125	Pd
	200.00			Pd.
	75.00			Pd
	250	50 –		Pd
	35.			Pd.
	115 –	40 –	75.00	Pd
	65.00		65 / 140.00 Pd 115.00 Bal 25.00	

REX COSTUMES
THEATRICAL WARDROBE
MADE ONLY TO
ORDER
NO RENTALS

Rex Huntington fitting a client in his studio.

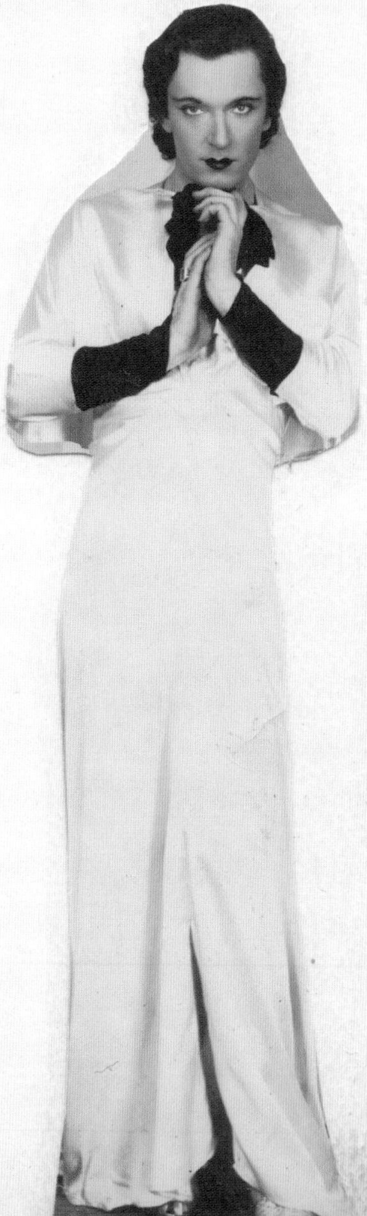

Rex's archive came to me through Joan Torino, one half of the "Toni Twins," an early 1950s act consisting of Joan and her friend Marie Collins. Joan and Marie were sixteen years old and looking for work when Joan's mother told them that the Hudson Theater in New Jersey was auditioning girls for the chorus line. Of course they lied to the manager, saying they were eighteen, and were hired on the spot.

The choreographer handpicked Joan and Marie to be "twins." Marie explained to me that she was the one who had to make all the alterations to her appearance in order to fit the billing: "Joan was taller than I was. So I had to do all the changes. She was a redhead. I was a brunette. So I bleached my hair to be a redhead. I made my heels higher, so I could hardly walk. And then, I met a guy that was like infatuated with me and he owned the fabric company. So he gave us the fabric. We proceeded to have the gowns made, ice blue with rhinestones."

The choreographer helped the girls develop a routine together, which Marie describes as such: "You know these are two baby pin spots [two small spotlights onstage]. She was in one. I was in another. And we'd go up to the microphone and . . . I would say, 'I'm the girl with the natural curl.' And Joan would get up and say, 'And I'm the girl with the Toni's. And she'd go bump. A whole part of our routine was taking this off at the same time, taking that off at the same time. But separate pin spots."

Marie eventually grew tired of stripping, got married, and now owns an inn in California. Joan had a longer career in burlesque, which she quit after a particularly bad experience while stripping in a nightclub. Though Joan left the burlesque stage, she remained in contact with many of her colleagues and developed an especially close relationship with costumer Rex Huntington. Rex left her his complete archive when he passed away in September 1992 at the age of eighty-five.

When Joan told me that she had some of Rex's sketches and costumes, I was certainly not expecting a literal timeline of burlesque costume design, circa 1916 to 1970, revealed through photographs, ledgers, and account logs of costumes made and sold. Rex's record books contain measurements for practically every major burlesque stripper of the twentieth century. His archive speaks volumes about the changes in public taste and morality through many eras of feminine silhouettes.

Rex was born in 1907 in Indiana. By the age of fourteen, he was

A flowing outer gown will leave an audience curious about what is worn beneath.

OPPOSITE PAGE:
Rex Huntington made these gowns for one of his female impersonator clients. Numerous burlesque queens have told me that once they tired of their gowns, they would sell them to drag performers, who were often the same size.

working as a chorus boy at the Hollywood theater in Detroit. An avid fan of the stage world, Rex collected professional 8 x 10 photographs of the chorus girls, burlesque comedians, and burlesque queens who stopped in Detroit to play the theater. He was particularly drawn to the costumes of the female performers, who, he realized, became immortalized through the stylization of their clothing and makeup. He regularly hung around the costume shop at the theater, admiring the work of the wardrobe mistresses, and eventually became head of wardrobe himself.

While Rex was creating costumes for burlesque queens, he had a parallel career working with female impersonators on their gowns and makeup. Many costume designers, including Jack of Hollywood and Gussie Gross, made wardrobes for men as well. This was actually a lucrative trade. Female impersonators and burlesque strippers both existed on the fringes of society. Drag, in a similar fashion to burlesque, deals with extremes of representation and sexuality. In the 1920s, drag introduced a new element of titillation and entertainment to café society. Barbette, the famed transvestite trapeze artist much admired by Jean Cocteau, brought an unclassifiable type of beauty to the stage of the Folies-Bergère in Paris.

Through exaggerated makeup and costume, transvestites embodied a newfound sexual freedom that echoed the current image of the liberated female "flapper." Transvestitism brought a sense of political and social satire to the stage, deeply tinged with sexual humor. In the nightclubs of Weimar-era Berlin, drag performance became symbolic of the decadence and decaying glamour of a city on the brink of apocalypse. "Grotesque" makeup and cleverly designed costumes helped disguise the sex of the performer.

In America, Julian Eltinge, a popular female impersonator in the early teens, was so admired for his elegant gowns and "feminine" grace that women and men alike flocked to the theaters to see him perform. He even had a Broadway theater named after him in 1912, the Eltinge, where many vaudeville and burlesque performers took the stage.

A sense of campy, yet classy sex appeal is evident in Rex's sketches, attesting to his work with both male and female clients. In his designs he strived for a mixture of elegance and gaudiness. He tutored his clients on the finer points of maintaining the proper burlesque persona—for instance, advising Bambi Vawn, a burlesque stripper known as "The Pocket-Sized Venus," not to wear jewels onstage unless they were real.

Rex was an expert at creating curves and hips where none existed. He used concealing fringes and panels to take away inches where they were unwanted, and added inches to the décolletage with padding and flesh-colored hoisting straps. Using lumberjack zippers, among other techniques, to ease the difficult operation of disrobing, he helped his clients strategize the most effective ways to remove their costumes.

From his early photographic collection of 1920s chorus girls and stripteasers to documentation of his wardrobe for Ann Corio's Broadway show, *This Was Burlesque*, Rex's archive conveys not only his talent as a costume designer, but also his admiration for the burlesque queens with whom he worked. Throughout the years I've spent documenting the lives and careers of the last great generation of burlesque queens, I have watched friends pass away and have often been frustrated by the amount of material that remains lost or neglected. Thankfully, Joan Torino has remained true to Rex long after his passing, and his accomplishment in burlesque costume design will see the light of day once more.

Sketch by Rex Huntington.

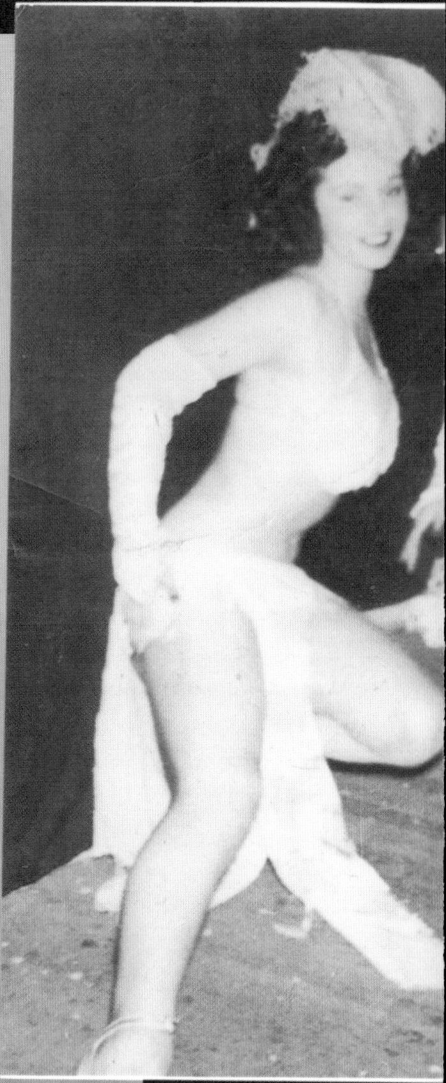

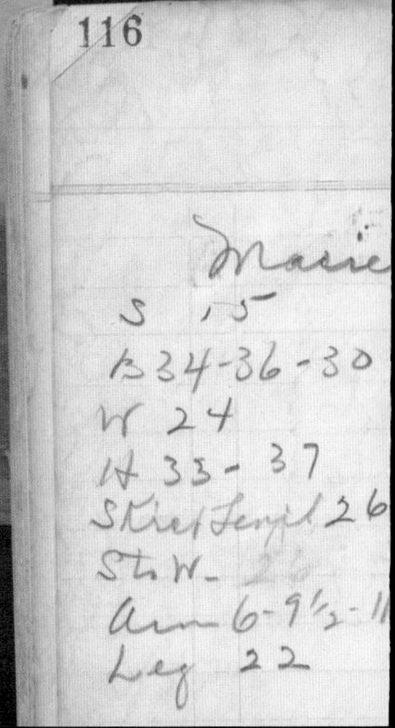
116

Marie
S 15
B 34-36-30
W 24
H 33-37
Skirt Length 26
St. W.
Arm 6-9½-11
Leg 22

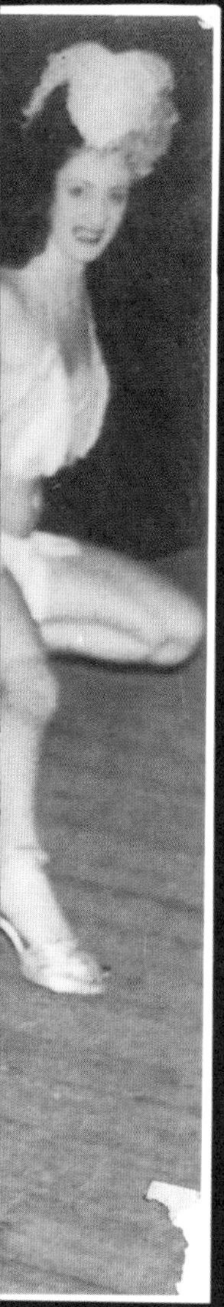

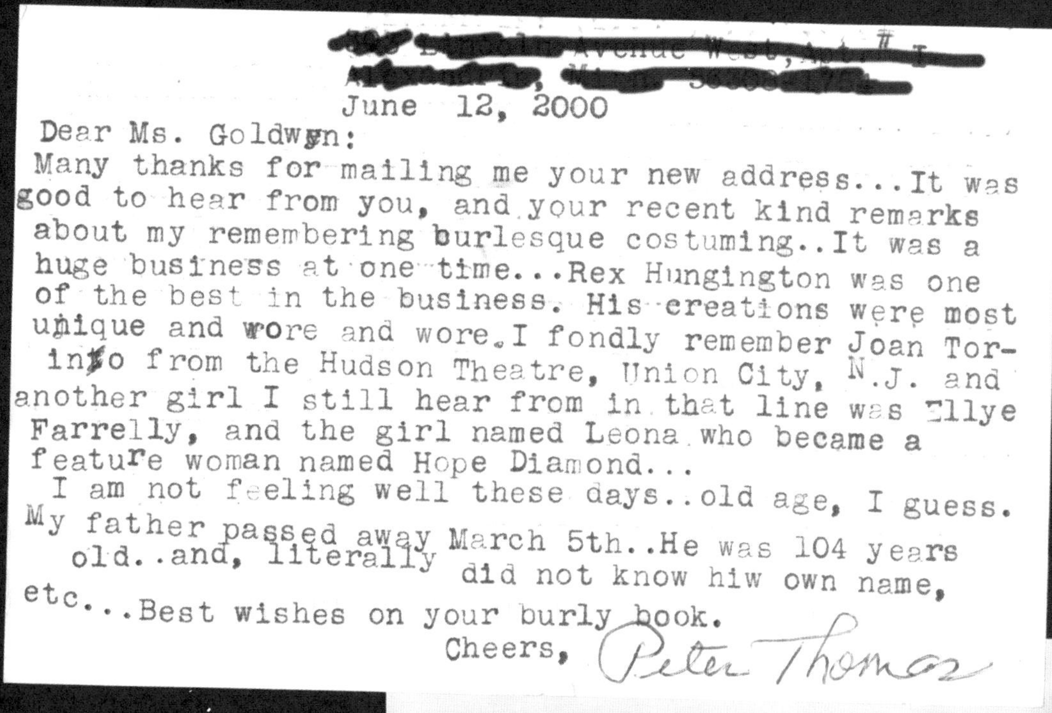

[redacted]

June 12, 2000

Dear Ms. Goldwyn:

Many thanks for mailing me your new address...It was good to hear from you, and your recent kind remarks about my remembering burlesque costuming..It was a huge business at one time...Rex Hungington was one of the best in the business. His creations were most unique and wore and wore. I fondly remember Joan Tor-ino from the Hudson Theatre, Union City, N.J. and another girl I still hear from in that line was Ellye Farrelly, and the girl named Leona who became a feature woman named Hope Diamond...

I am not feeling well these days..old age, I guess. My father passed away March 5th..He was 104 years old..and, literally did not know hiw own name, etc...Best wishes on your burly book.

Cheers, Peter Thomas

Like the Barrison Sisters before them, the Toni Twins did not have family ties.

ABOVE:
A correspondence that led me to Joan Torino and Rex Huntington's archives.

BELOW:
Joan and Marie's measurements from Rex's ledger.

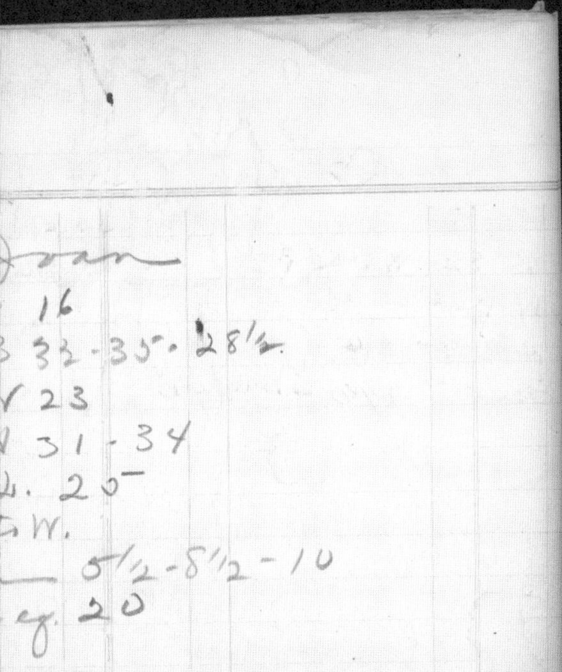

Joan
16
33-35-28½
23
31-34
20
5½-8½-10
20

When ordering, BE CERTAIN to fill in the following measurements for proper fit:

Garment for LADY ....✓...... or MAN ....

Height ..5 ft. 4"..... Bust or Chest ..37"........

Waist ..27"..... Hips ..36"..... Collar ..15"....

LONG WAISTED

Regular Dress Size ....

Between Shoulders at Back ..17"...................

FROM BASE OF COLLAR AT BACK:

Length of Dress .... or Gown ....

Length of Skirt - Waist to Hem ....

OTHER INFORMATION & SPECIAL INSTRUCTIONS

WAIST TO CROTCH - FRONT 12½" ....

.." ...." ANKLE BONE - OUTSIDE - 37"

CROTCH TO ANKLEBONE - INSIDE - 26"

SHOULDER TO WAIST - FRONT - 19½"

..." ... " ... " - BACK - 19¼"

...." ...." BOTTOM OF SLEEVES - 2

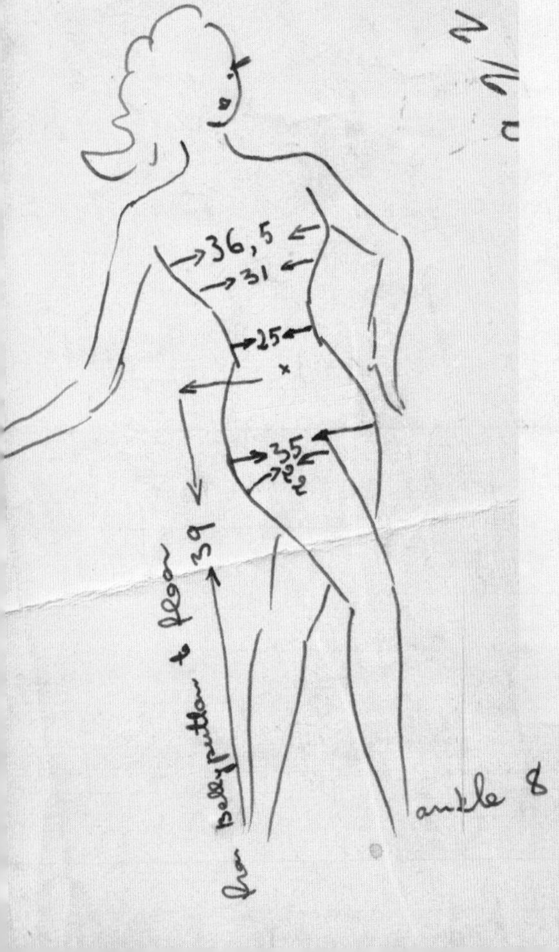

NOT ALLOW
TUCK-IN

Maurice Seymour

Rex's sensibilities leaned toward Vegas showgirl exuberance.

BLR lace

36 B
Circle underskirt
Panel
Padded
Push up
Hi jock-garter
Pink velvet
Pink Chiff
Electric
Blue
Delustered
Satin
Taffeta

COAT
OVER DRESS
This black design will be in white iris + hot pink sequins also white iris on top of coat
rest of coat is plain material
REX COSTUMES
287 PARK AVENUE
WEEHAWKEN, N. J. 07087
TEL. (201) UN 4-1248

PINK
~~WHITE~~
CHIFFON
SHORT
DRESS
Solid
hot pink
sequin
dress-with
white trim
HOT PINK + WHITE SEQUIN
GARTER
BELT
BRA
PANTS
G-STRING
BETWEEN
$800.00
$900.00
as designed
3
15
RED SEQUIN
BRA
PANTS
G-STRI
$385.0
as des
DRESS + COAT
MADE OF BONDED CREPE
LINED IN COMPATABLE
SHADE OF PINK
TOP OF COAT OFF WHITE CREPE
RETURN SKETCHES PLEAS

"Romayne & Moe" exemplify one version of the popular "man and woman act," in which costume was used to imply both sexes dancing together, usually ending with the "male" stripping the female of her attire.

To
"Rex"
From the
two of us
"Moe &
Romayne"
Bloom

In the 1930s and 1940s in the United States, burlesque shows were officially segregated, and most queens were Caucasian. It was considered "exotic" to include a performer of color on a bill. Lois de Fee told me that they had what they called "black and white" bills. She says, "They would have the complete white show with the white chorus girls and comics and the strippers. And then they would have a black show with a black chorus line and a black comic. Pigmeat Markham was the black comic, mostly best known in burlesque. But strippers they didn't have; black strippers they didn't have."

Lois was insistent that there were no black strippers, but there was one Asian queen she remembered: Mai Ling, pictured here. I gather from conversations I've had with other performners that Mai Ling is a racially mixed woman with some African-American blood, posing as "Asian" as part of her gimmick. I believe it was simply so unheard of to have a black performer on a white bill at that time that the same practice of blacks "passing" for whites went for burlesque performers at the time. Even backstage, dressing rooms and common areas of the time were segregated for black or white bills.

OPPOSITE PAGE: *Mai Ling's measurements.*

To Bernard Pat,
Love,
Mei Ling
Boris Bakchy
N.Y.C.
Mei Ling
S 14
B 35 38-30
W 28
H 34-36-37
SL. 41
ARM 5½ - 9½ - 10½ 19 - Length 23
Panels. 30 - 34 - 30
Skirt Length 43 -
Coat 58
neck 13
Stow - F 18 - B 18

SHO
TH

OPPOSITE PAGE:
A young Ann Corio.

THIS PAGE:
Showbill with Ann Corio on the cover. Rex created the entire wardrobe for burlesque queen Ann Corio's This Was Burlesque, *a stage show that looked back on the true golden period of this form of entertainment, remembering its queens, chorus girls, and comedians through sketches and song. The show opened in 1962 and ran for almost thirty years. Her book also titled* This Was Burlesque, *was published in 1968, and established Ms. Corio as a "legitimate" performer, using her striptease career as fodder to entertain the masses.*

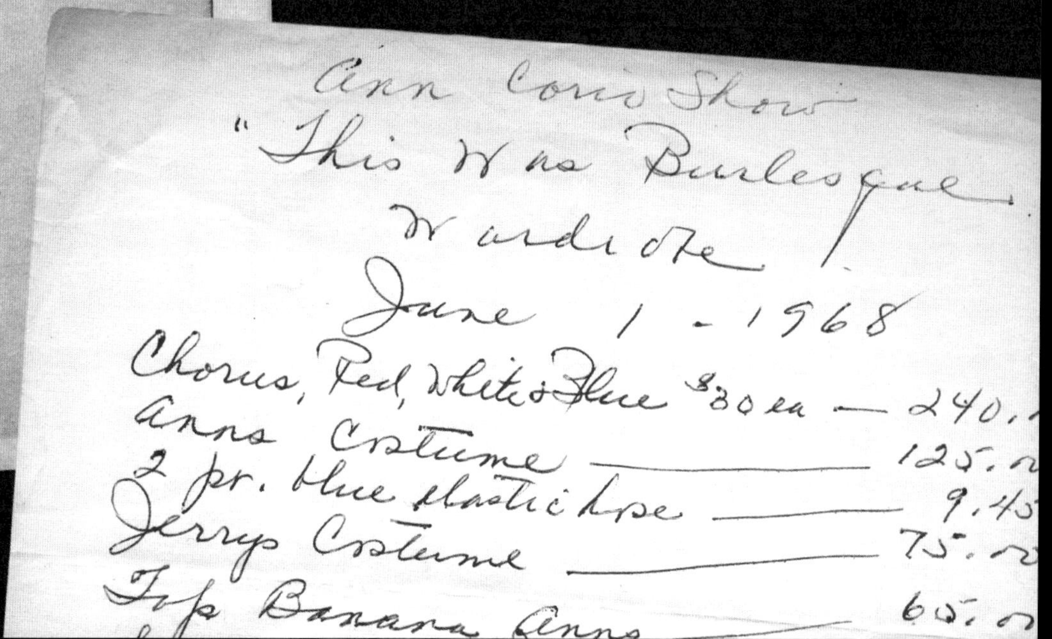
Ann Corio Show
"This Was Burlesque
Wardrobe
June 1 - 1968
Chorus, Red, White & Blue $30 ea — 240.
Anns Costume — 125.
2 pr. blue elastic hose — 9.45
Jerrys Costume — 75.
Top Banana Anns — 65.

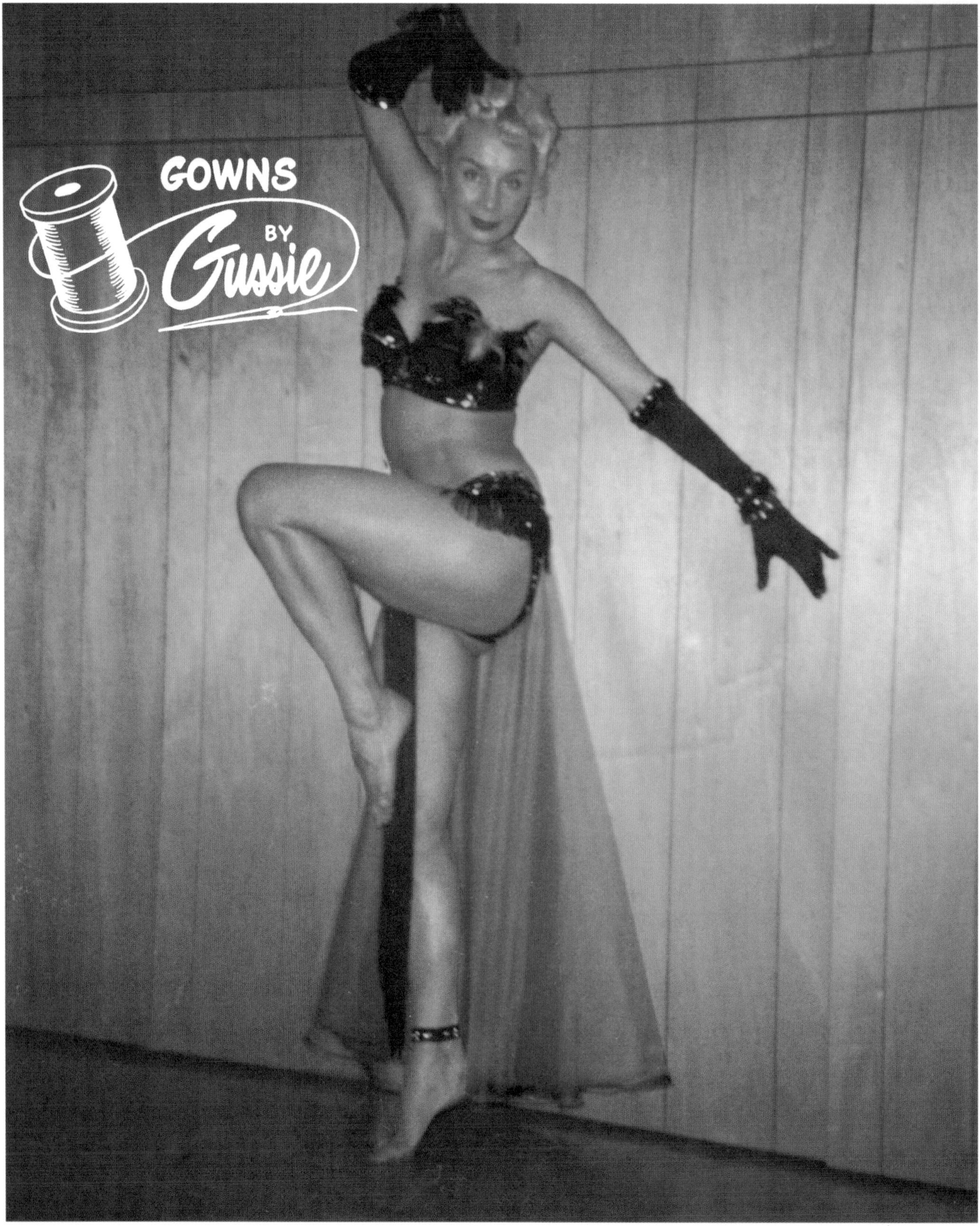
GOWNS
BY
Gussie

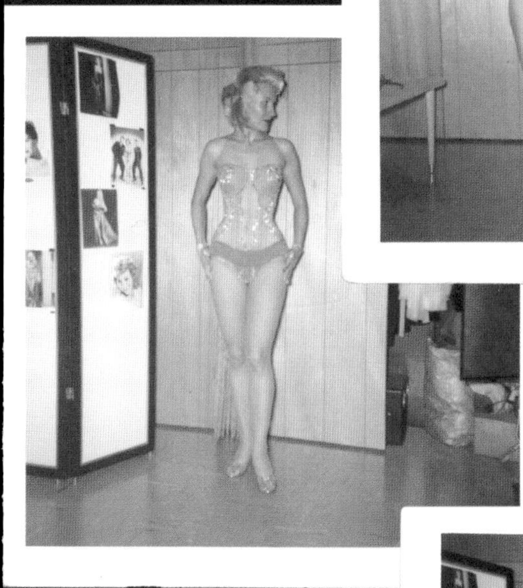

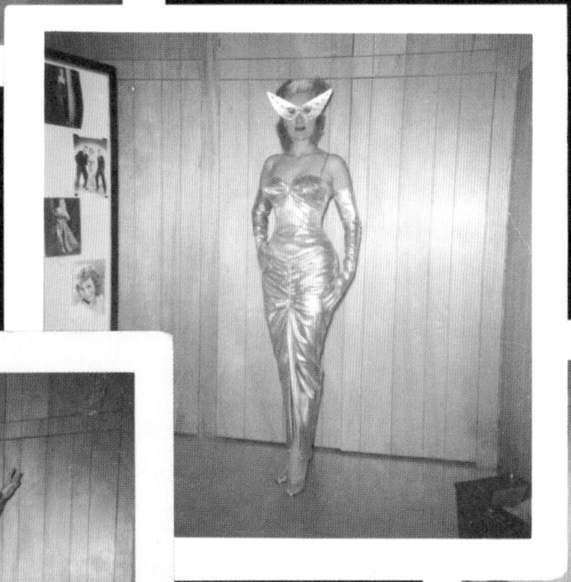

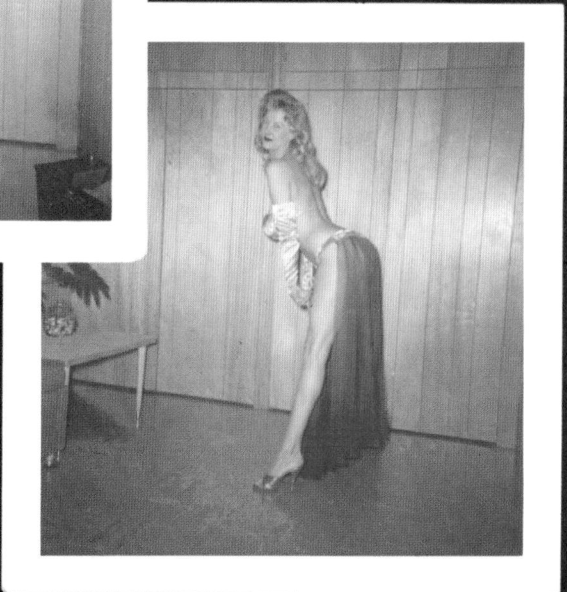

OPPOSITE PAGE:
Gussie's first husband, Ed Gross, introduced her costuming talents to the world of burlesque. After all, policemen themselves were fans of burlesque—note Ed's LAPD card with a prized autograph by Lili St. Cyr on its reverse side.

Gussie Gross was born Augusta Kollar in 1917 in Los Angeles. She made clothes for her dolls as a child and went to school to study fashion and pattern making at the age of sixteen. After graduating, Gussie worked for a designer named Bonnie Columbus in downtown Los Angeles, where she honed her skills making street clothes and evening wear for wealthy clientele. In the late 1930s, Gussie's creative spark turned to photography, and she became a staff photographer at the Star Studio of Hollywood.

At twenty, Gussie married her first husband, Ed Gross, who was a vice squad police officer. One day, he took her along with him to a raid on a burlesque club, the Follies, in downtown Los Angeles. He frequently had to arrest the strippers because they were always "forgetting" to wear pasties and G-strings under their costumes. The law in Los Angeles at this time was strict: all parts covered. But laws varied from town to town and many girls came from other states and cities. The legalities of acceptable "display" on the burlesque stages differs according to location; each state had its own rules, which varied from month to month, performer to performer. Some of the women I talked to who performed in Los Angeles in the 1930s and 40s told me that the New York girls who came out to perform at the Follies in L.A. would go without "proper onstage attire." They didn't have a law in New York at the time requiring pasties and G-strings, so the girls from back East would get everyone busted by the cops.

Of course, adherence to such legal ordinances also depended on whether or not the censors were in the audience on any given night. A red light in the orchestra pit signaled that the coppers were in attendance. When that light was off, it was a cue for the girls to "work strong"—flash a little, so to speak.

Everyone seems to have a different version of how far one could go onstage. Zorita, an extremely provocative queen, said that when she worked in Canada she wasn't allowed to stand still; she had to keep moving. The censors would come to the shows to make sure that the girls were abiding by the rules. Zorita described one altercation with the censors in Canada after they found fault with her routine: "I said, 'Well, my body is moving.' They said, 'Yes, but your feet have got to be moving, and don't touch yourself.' I said, 'My brassiere unhooks from the front . . . I unhook this bra, and I've got to put my hands between my breasts to unhook it.' 'Well, all right, but don't be getting cutzie-cutzies, and don't put your hands by your tush.' There were some places you had to wear flesh-colored net pants, but on the beach nowadays they're wearing the thong up the tush. You couldn't do that in burlesque."

Ed, who had firsthand knowledge of both the politics of the clubs and Gussie's talents as a seamstress, introduced her to the choreographer of the show, Lillian Hunt, who promptly hired her to make pasties and G-strings for the girls so they could keep out of trouble. When Hunt came to pick up the wares and saw the extensive wardrobe Gussie had created for her daughter's dance class, she begged her to create costumes for the girls as well.

Gussie was known for the intricate details and techniques of her costumes. Notes on her sketches mention embellishments such as pleated netting, horsehair, metallic braid, crystal drops, and fabric dye. Describing her gowns to me, Gussie said, "They were made so well . . . you never saw a raw seam inside. Everything was lined so they were as pretty inside as they were outside." In fact, lining was an important detail of burlesque costuming. As pieces came off and were turned inside out and flipped around as determined by the choreography, the interiors of the garments were revealed to the audience.

Many queens have told me that it was taboo to throw their wardrobes on the floor as they stripped. To avoid having their expensive gowns

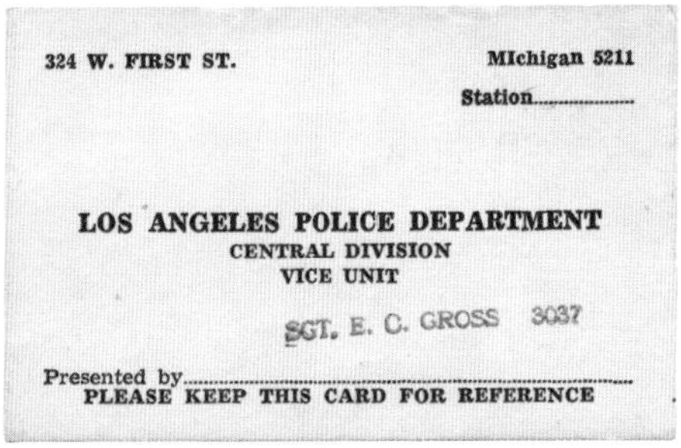

324 W. FIRST ST. Michigan 5211

Station..........

LOS ANGELES POLICE DEPARTMENT
CENTRAL DIVISION
VICE UNIT

SGT. E. C. GROSS 3037

Presented by..........
PLEASE KEEP THIS CARD FOR REFERENCE

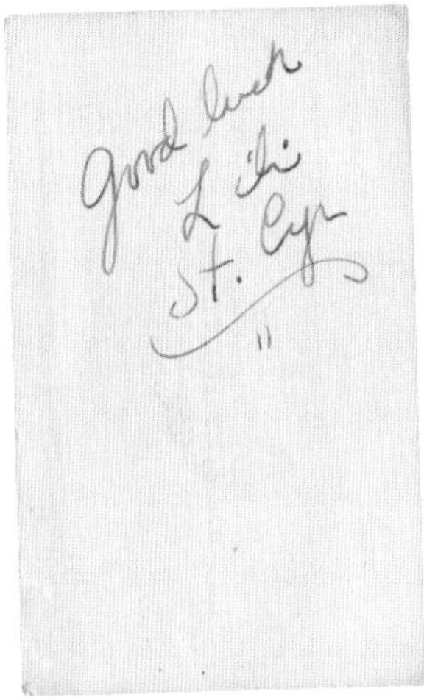

land on the dirty stage floor, the headliners would usually have their maids waiting in the wings or pay one of the chorus girls to catch their wardrobe for them. Joan Torino, who idolized Tempest Storm, used to catch her wardrobe when they were both were performing at the Hudson Theater in New Jersey.

Gussie sat night and day hand-sewing beads and sequins onto the costumes, working with the girls to create the right look for each of their acts—enhancing their assets and covering their flaws. Gussie says she would ". . . have a discussion with them about what their most appealing feature was, and like Busty Brown or Tempest Storm, they had such huge busts . . . And so, you know, accentuate the positive. . . . Most of the time they would ask me to come see their show so I would design something appropriate for their number."

At night Gussie observed her handiwork in action, checking for any faults with the wardrobe and making last-minute repairs. She loved to watch the show and was as much a part of the action as the performers were. I once asked her whether her experiences working with beautiful stripteasers affected her view of her own sexuality or body image. She responded that it never bothered her because "there was a transformation from the way they looked when they came here in the afternoon for a fitting to when they went on the stage . . . . I always figured I could hold my own with most of them because I wasn't a bad looking young lady."

Gussie estimates that she made roughly one thousand costumes over her twenty years in the business, with prices ranging from $200 to $500 depending on the value of the fabric and how many pieces were involved. To document her work, she took Polaroid photos of the girls in each piece of their costume (some costumes had as many as ten pieces) before it left her studio. The girls would reenact their stripteases in slow motion as Gussie captured their poses on film. Gussie pulled out hundreds of these images, grouped in sequences, the first time I visited her.

Many of her clients were unidentified women who saved up enough money to buy one Gussie original. Others were repeat customers whose Polaroid images tend to be peppered with babies, dogs, and various boyfriends. Though Gussie tried to be maternal with her "girls," she had a full roster to look after and many of them had sad stories to tell.

Tanayo, one of Gussie's clients known as "The Costa Rican Dream

TOP:
The Follies gang out to dinner. People at the table include (l-r) burlesque queen extraordinaire Lili St. Cyr, stage director and actor at the Follies Leon De Voe, choreographer Lillian Hunt, and Ed and Gussie Gross.

BOTTOM:
Sue Martin, burlesque queen, and Bob Biggs, owner of the Los Angeles Follies Theater, pose together backstage.

Street wear designed by Gussie Gross for a LAPD Fashion Show, modeled by policemen's wives.

Girl," was seventy-three years old when we became pen pals in 1999. She had cancer and found her condition unbearable, praying to God to make her better. Financially, she was in dire straits, unable to make do anymore with her sideline of selling bikinis to strip clubs—she said the clubs had gotten wise and put in their own boutiques. She started on the burlesque circuit in 1946 in New York City. Her heyday was in the 1950s and 60s, mostly working in California and a bit in Mexico. She had a daughter while she was at the height of her career and, according to another customer of Gussie's, she made many sacrifices for her daughter to have a good life—such as sending her to private schools. Gussie told me that "she was one of these kind, good little Catholic mothers" but Gussie found it funny that whenever Tanayo had a costume fitting, "there would be a gentleman in the front room sitting there waiting to pay for it." Tanayo and I exchanged letters for years until she couldn't write anymore. We finally met at Gussie's house during a reunion with some of the girls. It was to be the first and last time I saw her.

Another client of Gussie's with whom I've become friendly over the telephone and through letters went by the stage name "Nocturn." She is afraid to "come out" to her community as a former burlesque queen. So many years after the demise of burlesque, the word "burlesque" still carries negative connotations. Many queens have told me that when people find out about their past career, they are met with stares of shock and scorn. Nocturn is now a born-again Christian living in the Southwest. She tells me that no one in her community knows anything about her past. Believing that her religious peers would more readily accept AIDS and homosexuality than stripping, she equates Christianity to show business, saying that nobody wants anyone to get any "dirt" on them, for fear it might ruin their career.

Nocturn's father was a vaudeville and burlesque comedian known as "Laughing Lou Lamar," so she grew up seeing burlesque shows. In 1947, when she was about sixteen years old and performing in the chorus at the Roxy Theater in Cleveland, Ohio, she saw some of the last great burlesque queens, whom she considered "artists." One act that particularly impressed her was performed in a giant champagne glass. Nocturn took ballet class and always wanted to dance, but when she finally made it to the big city—Los Angeles—she was broke and started stripping to make ends meet. By the time she got into burlesque in the early 1950s, most shows were in nightclubs, and socializing with customers was a focal point of the business.

Nocturn hated drinking with the customers and receiving propositions from drunken lechers. In the theater, customers were not allowed backstage or anywhere near the girls at all. In nightclubs, however, the girls were expected to sip drinks in tight cocktail dresses with the audience after their acts. Nocturn says she became an alcoholic to deal with her profession and it almost ruined her.

Joan Torino told me the following story about the only evening she ever worked in a nightclub, which seems to sum up the general degradation of burlesque from a popular form of theatrical entertainment to the contemporary strip club environment we know today:

LIZ: What was it like when you stripped in the nightclubs?

JOAN: I only worked one night. I didn't like it. I didn't like having to drink. I didn't like having to sit with somebody . . . It was just too intimate. I didn't like alcohol around the stripping, myself.

LIZ: How forward would men get with their advances in the nightclub?

JOAN: I was having some champagne and when it became my turn to go up and strip, [the man I was sitting with at a table] he says, when you come down, leave your pants up there. And I said, why? And I'm still trying to figure it out. Well, there was white tablecloths, I guess, so he could fool around under the table.

LIZ: How had it changed?

JOAN: So, I quit. The art was thoroughly gone. I mean, you were just like dancing, drinking, you know? Which was an honest living. I'm not saying there was anything wrong with that, but it wasn't the theater that I was used to.

Gussie Gross's sentiments about the end of her career are echoed in this 1960s cartoon.

As go-go dancing came into vogue and skimpy costumes became the norm, there was little work left for costume designers like Rex and Gussie. When Gussie's grandson asked her why she quit designing, she answered, "When burlesque went topless, I lost half of my business, and when it went bottomless it put me out of business."

But by the time burlesque was on its way out, these designers had helped to create many larger-than-life stars, and their costumes and ideas survive to this day.

A good example of a fishnet bodysuit with jeweled bra, tassels, and panties sewn onto the net to cover this dancer's assets.

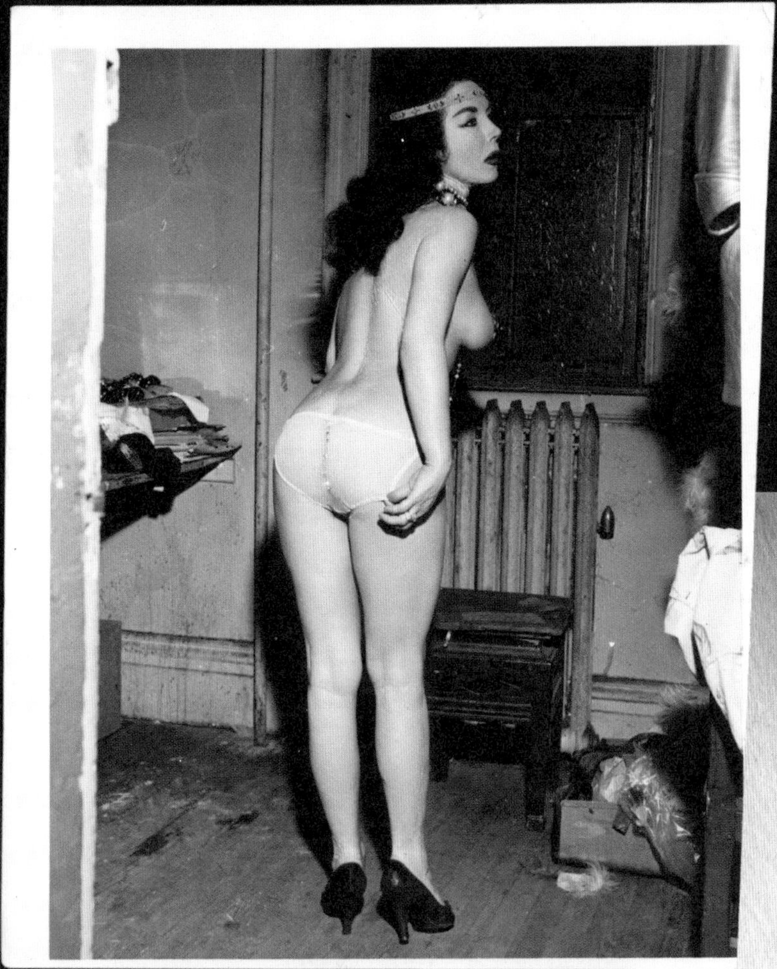

Gussie recalls, "The law was very strict in those days. The girls . . . had to wear pasties and they had to wear these little panties that had fabric in the front covering the pubic hair and a strip up the back not showing the crack in the—I guess you call it the 'buns.' So, that [making pasties and G-strings] got me started in a very lucrative business."

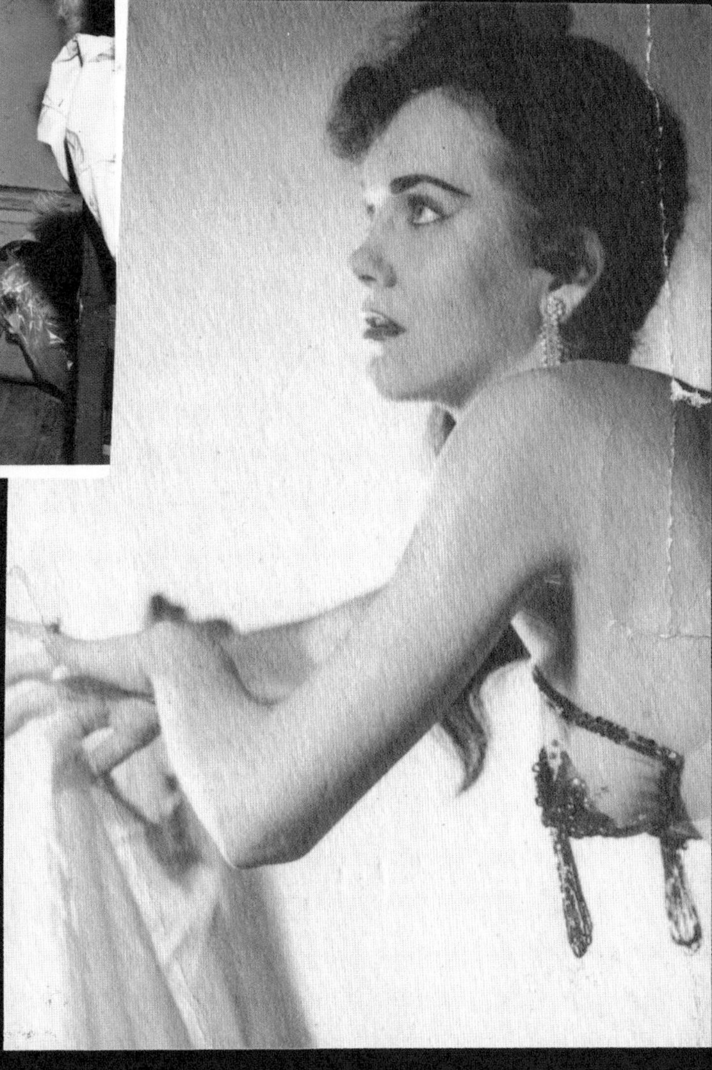

Ruthie Lewis, a former client and close friend of Gussie's, with long tassels dangling from her pasties. The trick of "tassel twirling" (whereby the girls made tassels on the end of their pasties swing in different directions) was made easier by attaching a fish swivel to the pasties to give the tassels weight.

ORCHID GOWN

X CLEAN GOWN ✓X
X NEW PETTICOATS ✓X
X NEW PANEL ✓X
NEW GLOVES ✓
X DYE FRINE DK OR.
X NEW FRINGE BRA X

AQUA BEADED GOWN

X AQUA GOWN-BEADED ✓X
NEW X BLACK TULLE COAT X
NEW X BLACK LACE TEDDY X
X BR AQUA FRINGE BRA (AND FRINGE)

BLACK LACE GOWN

✓ ~~NEW~~ BLACK LACE GOWN

X ALTERNATE WITH BLACK TULLE COAT. OR X

X TULLE GLOVES,

~~BLACK TEDDY~~ ?

BLACK SLIP ?

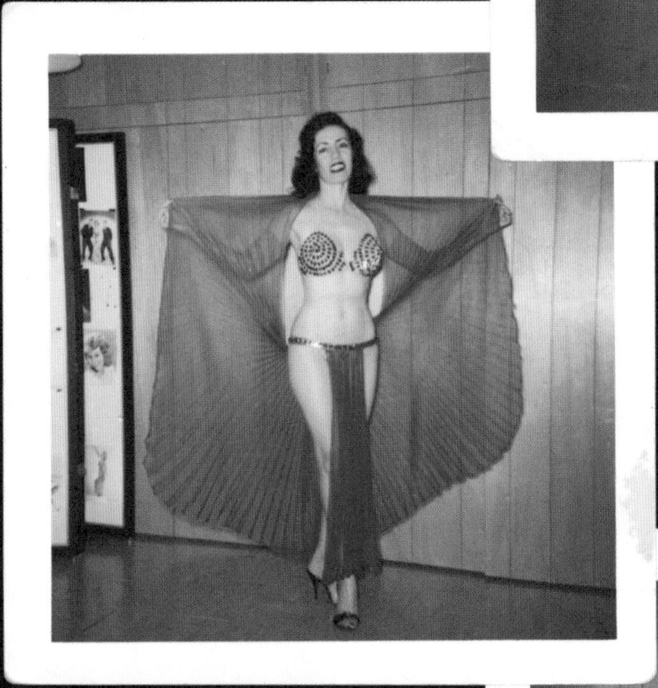

Tanayo reveals the layers of her orchid gown.

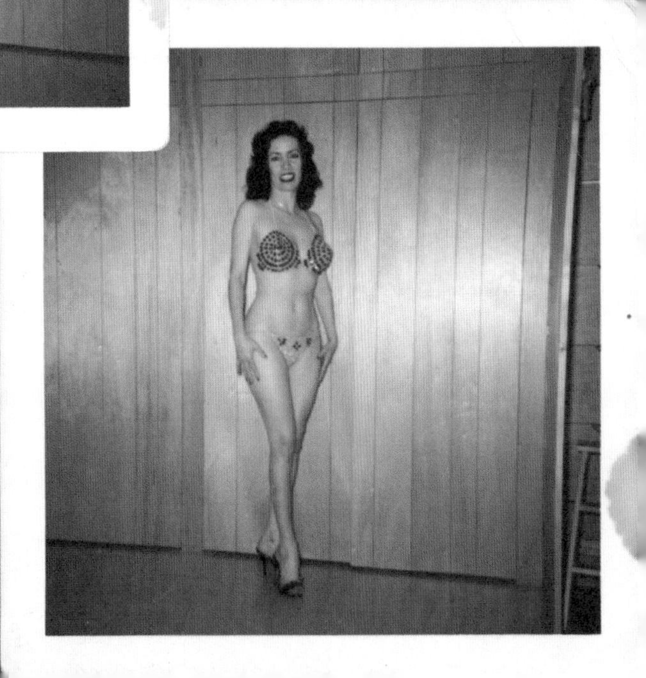

WHITE BEADED GOWN

✓ NEW WHITE BEADED GOWN (SILVER + RED)

X NEW RED TULLE DUSTER

X WHITE TEDDY

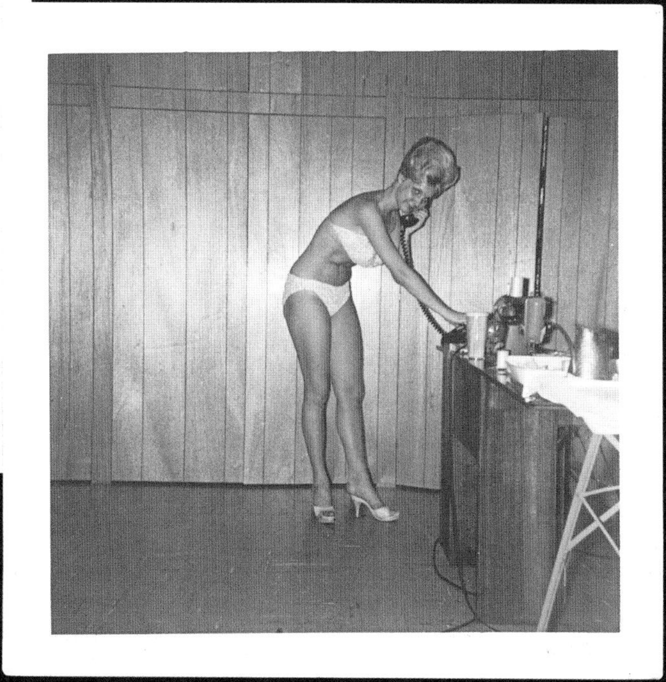

Gussie regularly took Polaroids of various clients wearing her completed designs.

Garbo
CHICAGO

GUSSIE GROSS:
This is Rene Andre, she was one of the first gals that ever had bust surgery and it was terrible.

LIZ:
Why was it terrible?

GUSSIE GROSS:
Well because they didn't do the surgery like they do now, you know, underneath where there's no scar. They just split the nipple and oh she suffered something terrible. She almost died.

Rusty Lane was known as the "The Duchess of Dis-Robe."

In this Polaroid taken by Gussie Gross, Rusty Lane wears one of Gussie's favorite creations. An eye-popping extravaganza, this lavender gown had hand-beaded fringe from top to bottom and four-inch beaded tassels on the bra underneath waiting to be revealed.

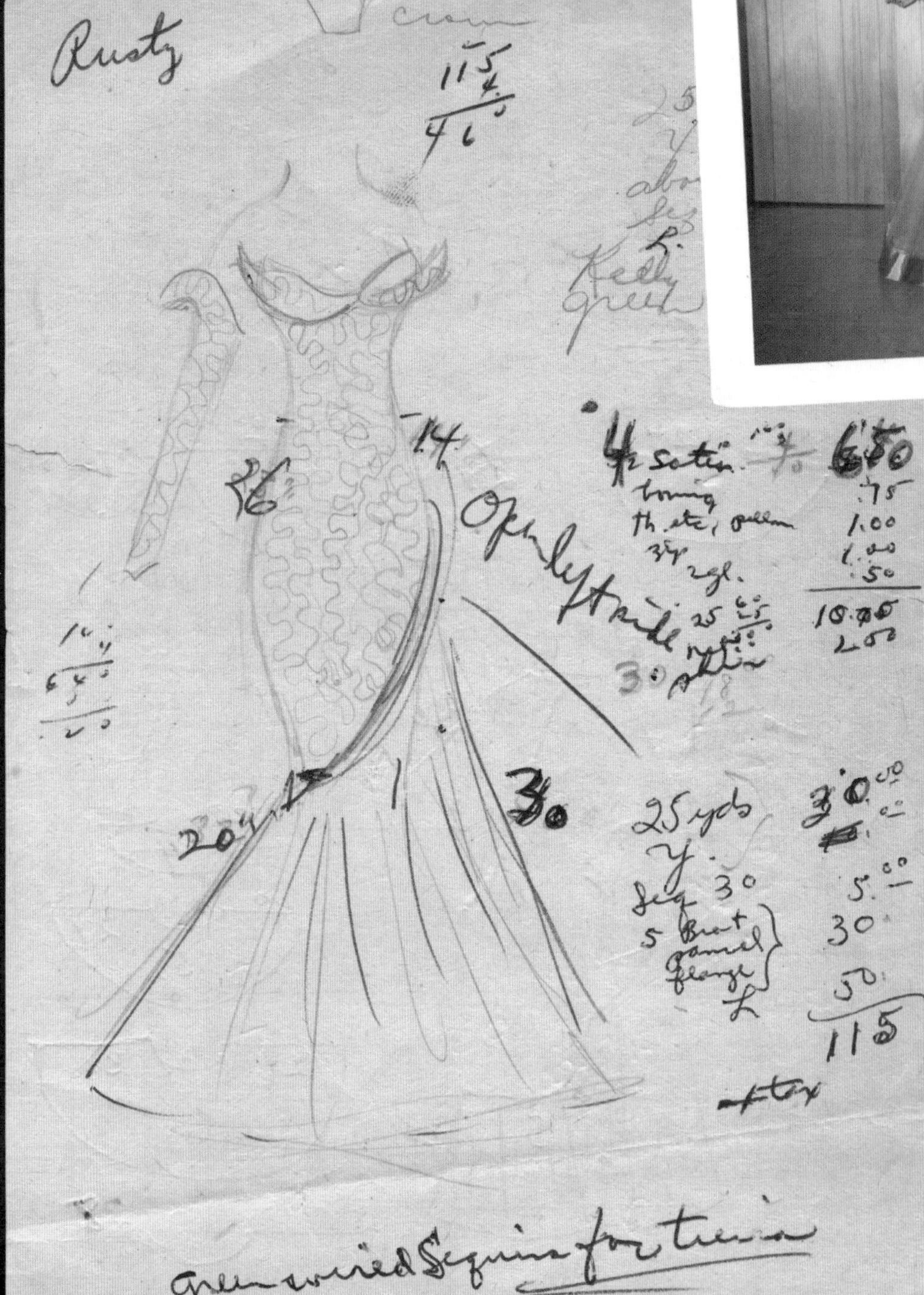

Jan. 58

WHIT
X WASH STEAM
X Feathered
X FEATHERED
ALTERNATE
X FUSHIA FR
X AQUA FRI
X RED FRING
X BLACK FRIN
NEW X BLUE FRIN
WHITE FRI

Jan. 58
EMERGENCY
FIRE DOOR
Only
DO NOT USE

RED SATIN
✓ NEW RE
✓ ADD FEAT
✓ REMODL H
X RED FRIN

Patti Waggin was one of Gussie's favorite clients. Here she wears the green "Africuban" and white "Africuban" costumes as sketched in Gussie's notebook.

Gussie's sketch for Nocturn's elaborate costume and headpiece.

TOP: *Nocturn in the realized costume.*

BOTTOM: *Nocturn poses in her new costume outside Gussie's Los Angeles home.*

Nocturne

Gussie fitting Nocturn in her studio.

Onstage

The stagehands and cast members backstage at the Follies Theater, Los Angeles.

Chorus girls with nice gams at the Hollywood Theater in Detroit, where Rex Huntington started his career as a chorus boy and Paul Morokoff was in-house choreographer.

Because people were not allowed to bring cameras inside burlesque theaters to record performances, there is a common misconception that the shows consisted of a series of strip routines presented against a drab backdrop of stage curtains. The archival film footage that does exist features women dancing at eye level with the camera, as if there were no audience. This is because queens were sometimes paid for private performances and recorded by enterprising men who then screened the films at stag parties or sold copies via mail order. Since these films are not true to the authentic burlesque performances in the theater, one must consider the entire production to get a full picture of how they were staged.

The opening numbers of a show usually included a comedian's introduction of the cast and chorus girls, and a "talking scene" in which burlesque queens and comedians performed together as foils. Scenery included backdrops and props relevant to the material, which often poked fun at police officers, boys' nights out on the town, or popular cultural figures such as judges and politicians. Burlesque queen Sherry Britton describes one talking scene she did with comic Tommy Mulraft: "It was a barroom scene. And what I did was to go over to the bar, and pick up two large glasses, fill them with water, take a deep breath, and I didn't wear a bra, so it shows you the quality of my body, and I put one glass on each breast, and I walked slowly and very carefully across the stage. And I got a lot of attention, a lot of applause."

Burlesque queen Ruthie Lewis poses backstage at the Follies Theater, Los Angeles, against her personal backdrop, in a costume by Gussie Gross.

Each week the theater featured a different comic and star, so performers learned quickly about timing and playing off the audience. Sherry tells another story in which Tommy Mulraft reacted to a man in the audience and subsequently coined a new slang term. She explains, "If a comedian became upset with someone in the audience, like this little Tom Mulraft, he called him a jerk. At that time, that word . . . was a street term for masturbation, so that it was very shocking. Now, it's part of our language." Sherry goes on to comment that "anybody in burlesque that did scenes, particularly the men, were never at a loss."

After the opening number came a beginner stripper, followed by a series of comic sketches and the first elaborate chorus girl "extravaganza." The headlining burlesque queen would not make her first appearance until midway through the show, just before act two. Many of the queens traveled with their own backdrops, settees, or screens for their acts—whatever was required.

Others performed without any props beyond the stage curtains and the accompanying orchestra, in which case their wardrobe became essential to the act's success. Betty Rowland explains, "As a rule, the dance director would ask what color you were wearing at the start of the show and they would use that color through the show . . . The drape in back of you, the curtain that you worked in front of must be a contrast to your costume. If you're going to wear a blue costume you don't want to have a blue curtain in back of it. You want more of a beige curtain probably, or, if you're in all white [then a] nice black, darker curtain."

The second act of a burlesque show usually opened with the chorus girls, followed by more comedic routines, the last strip by the headliner, and the grand finale. In the finale, the star queen appeared surrounded by all the chorus girls. Zorita described one of her early appearances for which she was the centerpiece of the closing number—up in a prop moon: "I didn't know you were supposed to wait for somebody to bring a ladder to get you down out of it. I stepped over backwards and fell down . . . sixteen steps. [There were] eighty girls that [stood below me at my] feet."

The twentieth-century burlesque chorus girls were similar in concept to the Ziegfeld Follies Girls, a changing troupe of stunning women created by the great Broadway impresario Florenz Ziegfeld. Ziegfeld was notorious for his ability to assemble a bevy of beauties who promised stimulation and, in lieu of straightforward sexuality, an elegant air of romantic appeal. The Ziegfeld Girls' physical beauty attracted the male audience, while their fashionable costumes, elaborate sets, and lighting appealed to female viewers. Expensive costumes hinted at nudity, making the female form more tantalizing than titillating. Ziegfeld trolled the couture salons of London and Paris for inspiration, hiring designer Lucile, a.k.a. Lady Duff Gordon, to create clothing for his girls. Ziegfeld spared no expense in wardrobe, and employed top costumers such as Charles LeMaire, Raphael Kirchner, James Reynolds, and John Harkrider, who fashioned over-the-top headdresses made from the finest feathers and pearl trimming.

Scenery was equally elaborate in Ziegfeld productions. In 1915, he hired Joseph Urban to oversee backdrops and lighting. Urban even developed his own color in designing Ziegfeld scenery—"Urban blue"—which was used for sky effects. As Miles Kruger, founder and director of the Institute of the American Musical, puts it, Ziegfeld "was a man who understood that the more you give the audience, the higher you aspire to create beautiful images and beautiful moments, the more the audience will respond, and so the better the box office will be . . . Ziegfeld knew how to blend commerce and beauty."

Ziegfeld was a master at bringing burlesque "uptown" and often featured cleaned up burlesque jokes and comics. Fanny Brice, a burlesque comedienne who started on the Lower East Side telling ethnic jokes to immigrant audiences, became one of the brightest stars of the Ziegfeld Follies.

Lois de Fee, who was known for her ladylike, "Ziegfeld-type" strip, refers to burlesque as "the poor man's Ziegfeld." I once asked her to explain the difference between a Ziegfeld production and a burlesque show, and she answered, "A couple of million dollars . . . The [Ziegfeld chorus] girls might not have stripped, but they walked around darn close to it with those beautiful feathers tickling them."

The most famous burlesque queen, Gypsy Rose Lee, worked for Florenz Ziegfeld shortly before his death in his 1932 revue *Hot-Cha!* In 1936, she costarred in the Ziegfeld Follies, produced by Ziegfeld's wife Billie Burke, and had a talking scene where she lifted her skirt and played the cymbals between her knees.

Perhaps due to her training ground as a Ziegfeld performer, it was important to Gypsy that her shows appealed to both male and female audiences. Thus she created a similar format for her chorus girl troupe, adding her burlesque sensibility to the mix. In 1942 Mike Todd and Gypsy, as uncredited coproducer, opened the musical revue *Star and Garter*, which brought burlesque production mainstream. Hollywood costume designer Irene Sharaff designed the costumes for the show, which were executed by Ballet Russes' wardrobe mistress

Karinska. Gypsy took the costumes and production design of the Ziegfeld Follies and added tawdry humor, beautiful girls, music, dance, and live warm flesh.

With her quick wit and attention to detail, Gypsy was able to give burlesque a depth that other strippers could not. Sherry Britton says, "Gypsy was a story unto herself. First of all, she had financial backing from a man named Waxey Gordon [a gangster], which nobody has ever mentioned. And so, she was in a position of being financially secure, so that she could dictate. Plus the fact, she happened to be terribly bright with a very good sense of humor about stripping."

Whereas Ziegfeld Girls were more restrained in their sexuality, Gypsy's shows featured the women whom men wanted to sleep with but not necessarily take home to their mothers. In one number, aimed to poke fun at typical female gender roles, Gypsy's chorus girls portrayed different characters with costumes to match. These included the Devil, all hot and bothered in a deep red net and sequin costume; the Virginal Eve, who wore strategically placed fig leaves; and the Southern Belle, gentile and pure in white net and fringe with matching parasol.

For her finale number in *Star and Garter*, Gypsy took the stage with her army of chorus girls, against a backdrop painted with large stars. She paraded down a set of stairs, and performed her finale number, "We're the Star and Garter Girls," giving the audience a final dose of burlesque staging at its best.

From the simplistic to the extravagant, staging seamlessly fit the burlesque queens' strips into robust shows that thrilled and entertained audiences from coast to coast.

Betty Rowland performs onstage with chorus girls, and solo at the Follies Theater in Los Angeles.

OPPOSITE PAGE:
Man in the balcony watches the girls peel it off.

A number called "The Girl in the Police Gazette" from the show Star and Garter, *which opened June 24, 1942, at the Music Box Theater in New York City and closed December 4, 1943. Police officers appear in a burlesque sketch as a comic foil—often mirroring real scenes at the burlesque theater.*

#130 Finale -
Pink Feather Parade
Bob Carney Co
Week Oct 8th/37
Road #7

THIS, OPPOSITE, AND FOLLOWING PAGES:
Examples of elaborate burlesque chorus girl production numbers, inspired by Ziegfeld mise-en-scenes. *Staged by Paul Morokoff at the Hollywood Theater in Detroit.*

Silver Gate Ballet – Feb. 21st
Blk Drop in 3. – silver legs on it
2 set pc. in 1 – Diff. color lights
Black Arch leg in back of gate on side
Arch on 6ft – Blk in full

#138 Winter Stock - #1
Jan 28th 1938
opening set
Orange + Red Ruffle set.

arch set - Jan 17th/36
Lights Out
12 Girls Parade
Great Waltz set

THE NATION
PAT. REG. U.S.A.
POLIC
HELENE HUDSON
IRIS MARSHALL
CYNTHIA CAVANAUGH

R. L.
RUTH JOSEPH
LYNN POWERS
ADELE JERGENS
AUDREY WESTPHALL

Opening No.
"We're the Stars of Garter Girls"
(Photo taken before I joined show)
Gypsy in Centre

BY THE SEA
YVONNE KUMMER
ME
GARY MYLES
JOSINE CAGLE

Anita Arden:

Portrait of a Chorus Girl

Through a contact at the Costume Institute at the Metropolitan Museum of Art, I became pen pals with a woman in London named Anita Middleton, who had been one of Gypsy Rose Lee's star chorus girls under the stage name Anita Arden. She was in poor health and her eyesight was bad, so for the most part we communicated through her friend Sara Murphy, a young mother who had befriended Anita in a launderette and was enthralled by her stories of life on the road as a stripper. Through Sara, Anita sent me her scrapbooks containing photos and documents with detailed notes posted onto the images. She hoped that her stories would be preserved for posterity; she was eighty-two years old and doctors had told her she had six months to live.

Anita was born in 1917 in the Bronx, New York. An only child, she lived with her parents and grandmother in a two-bedroom apartment. When Anita was fifteen her father died of tuberculosis, and Anita's mother—too poor to support her child alone—moved in with one of her sisters and sent Anita to live with an aunt in Staten Island.

Anita got her first job working as a secretary for ten dollars a week in Manhattan. On her third day of work, she saw a newspaper advertisement calling for tall girls to audition for Billy Rose at his new theater, Casino de Paris—which much later became the nightclub Studio 54. Rose hired Anita as a showgirl with a starting salary of forty dollars a week. With her new earnings, Anita was able to move her mother, grandmother, and herself into a furnished apartment on Fifty-third Street in Manhattan. She was all of eighteen years old.

Anita said that Billy Rose (who, in addition to being a producer and theater owner, was also a lyricist and composer) didn't like her much because she was a brunette—apparently he liked blondes—and she couldn't sing. Anita was relegated to the chorus, though she enjoyed a brief stint as leading lady when the gangster boyfriend of the

Anita's mother pictured with Gypsy and Gypsy's son, Erik Preminger. Anita's mother was Gypsy's dresser and toured on the road with the troupe.

OPPOSITE PAGE:
Anita in her "Southern Belle" costume.

star pulled his girl out of the show and picked Anita as her replacement.

In 1935 Billy produced a circus-themed musical revue titled *Jumbo* at the Hippodrome Theater. Anita again played a showgirl, in a cast that included burlesque comedian Jimmy Durante, and rode a horse wearing a white feather bikini. During her run in the show, Anita met and became friends with Gypsy Rose Lee. Their relationship would prove important for her career and her future.

Anita kept a busy working schedule. In between gigs in Broadway shows, she found work in nightclubs such as the Stage Door Canteen as a showgirl, and did some modeling on the side—even posing for pinup artist Alberto Vargas in his 1948 calendar. Though she didn't like performing in nightclubs and mingling with the customers after her routine, she needed the money to support her family.

From 1936 to 1937 Anita appeared at the Paradise nightclub in New York. Her vital statistics are listed on the back of a photo taken there: height 5'11", bust 33.5", waist 24.5", hips 35", green eyes, and brown hair. It is easy to envision the legions of stage door Johnnies she must have acquired. ("Stage door Johnny" was a term coined in the Ziegfeld days for the men—many of them wealthy and married—who lined up outside the backstage doors waiting for the girls to leave the theater.) Her social life was supplemented by wealthy boyfriends like actor Tyrone Power, who could afford to take her out to nightspots such as the Stork Club and El Morocco, where she palled around with fellow showgirl friends Adele Jergens and Bunny Waters. From 1937 to 1938, Anita played one of the "scandal girls" in the revue *Three Waltzes* at the Majestic Theater. In 1942 Anita appeared at Billy Rose's Diamond Horseshoe, a nightclub in the basement of the Paramount Hotel in New York City. In the finale number, Anita was a vision in a pale pink chiffon and net gown with pale green and blue sequin embroidery. Other notable jobs include *Strip for Action* at the National Theater in 1942, where she was a replacement, and *Mexican Hayride*, produced that same year by Mike Todd at the Winter Garden and the Majestic. Anita was again a showgirl, joining a cast that included Gypsy Rose Lee's sister June Havoc.

In 1942 Gypsy cast Anita in her revue *Star and Garter* as one of the lead chorus girls. Anita played the Southern Belle character. Gypsy would actually stitch up this costume herself each night just before Anita went onstage and then cut her out of it afterward. Gypsy was a hands-on producer and performer who attended to every detail.

Anita's mother traveled on the road with her as Gypsy's dresser. It was not unusual for burlesque tours to become family affairs; in fact, Gypsy's son Erik Preminger (whose father was the famed director Otto Preminger) traveled on the road with his mother, privy to the very secretive backstage life. Anita toured with Gypsy in *Star and Garter* across the United States and the two traveled together to Europe to boost troop morale during and after World War II as well. Gypsy became a role model for Anita, showing her by example that women did not have to be relegated to the scenery. Like so many other women, Anita aspired to have a career like Gypsy's, but somehow she seemed destined to remain in the background, supporting the star acts.

During one stopover in London, Anita met the man she was later to marry, Guy Middleton, a well-educated actor who shunned his privileged background by pursuing theater. Seven years later, thirty-two years old, and still performing in nightclubs and receiving unwanted advances from the patrons, Anita decided she needed to find a husband. With Guy in mind, she left New York for London to track him down. They married in 1949 and settled into a large flat on St. James Place.

Guy was not the dream husband that Anita had envisioned; he failed to find a steady job once his acting work stopped paying the bills. Anita's mother was living with them at the time, and unbeknownst to Anita, Guy wrote to the British government that he couldn't support his American mother-in-law. She was soon deported.

Needing to earn more money to support her family, Anita turned to Gypsy, who helped find her some film work. Though they were uncredited bit parts, Anita appeared in *Babes in Bagdad* in 1952, which starred Gypsy, and in *Malaga* in 1954—both were filmed in Spain. Anita's squeaky voice and strong Bronx accent prevented her from getting any lines. When Guy urged Anita to quit the business (perhaps because he was jealous of her acting work), she did so without question and spent her days socializing and sewing in England instead.

Anita's mother died in January of 1973, and then Guy died in March the same year, deep in debt without even a savings account. While cleaning out his dressing room after his death, Anita found hidden photos of old girlfriends posing naked hidden underneath the carpet. Regardless of his cadlike behavior, Anita was still madly in love with Guy and was willing to forgive him anything. She sold everything that reminded her of Guy, and wrote in her diary daily about how much she missed him.

Anita died in May 1999. She had been preparing to die for the last twenty-odd years of her life. Her main concern had been leaving nothing and no one behind. Without children, her only legacy would be her career, which, in her lifetime, she did not see recognized. Anita's treasured scrapbooks now reside at the New York Public Library for the Performing Arts, ensuring that her heritage and contribution to the history of burlesque will not be forgotten.

A page from Anita Arden's scrapbook.

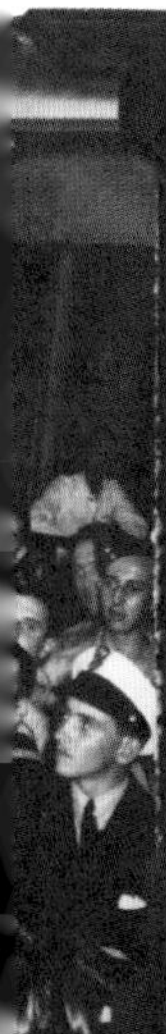

WHO'S YOUR FRIEND?

GREENWICH, CONN.

AT THE STAGE-DOOR CANTEEN.

MILDRED HUGHES LORRAINE LATHAM MIMI BERRY RUTHE REIDE ME

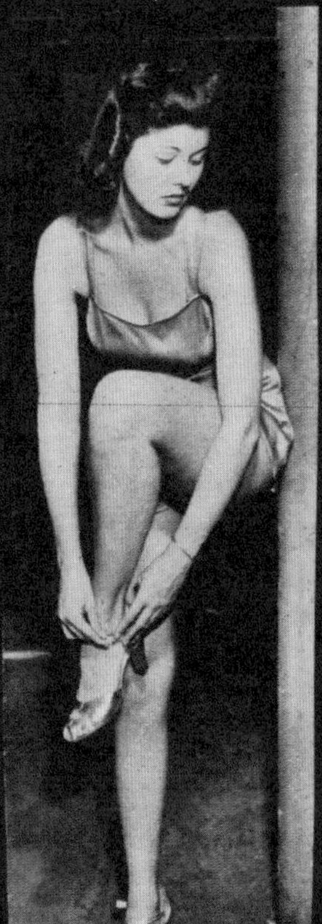

Gypsy's girls backstage as they prepare to go onstage in Berlin, 1938.

(Blonde hair for couple years!)
Not my own costume;
Gypsy tried this one
for me; liked the
white ("Southern Belle"
with parasol, better.
(This one: "Eve" of Helen Thomas)

Anita Arden

with Gypsy Rose Lee on Tour
1947, U.S
(31 yrs old)

- AT THE FROLICS, CHICAGO -

"SABLE"
(below)

She also had a 10 ft. long Sable Cape which she wore with Blue Jeans & Gold sandals. (High heels, of course!) First person I knew who wore gold shoes with Jeans.

In her dressing room she threw the cape on the floor for her tiny dog to lie on. Now,

that's STYLE!

ME

OPPOSITE PAGE:
Gypsy and her girls in the preshow huddle.

Gypsy made all these costumes *on* us — we had to stand for *hours*! Sequins pinned, then sewed, on "fish-net" stockings.

Green was "Eve"
Red – "She-Devil"
Gold – "Lady Godiva"
White – "Southern Belle"

NY

Dance
Empire
L. A.

To break the monotony of endless "bump 'n' grinds" and establish star reputations, burlesque queens removed their clothing with stylish and graceful moves. Unlike contemporary pole dancers, burlesque queens danced while wearing heavy costumes, and made it appear as if it were the easiest task in the world to provocatively remove gloves, cape, or gown. Though some women entered careers in burlesque with a dance background, many were just looking for work with two left feet.

I once asked Zorita, a notorious burlesque queen with outstanding acts, if she had ever taken dance classes as a child. She replied, "No, no. I just liked to dance. I used to put on the phonograph and dance around naked in the living room. . . . but they [her adoptive parents] never gave me dancing lessons. If they would have given me ballet or something, I probably wouldn't have wound up in burlesque."

THIS PAGE AND OPPOSITE:
Choreographers work out steps with burlesque dancers and chorus girls.

When a burlesque producer hired girls for the chorus, it was the job of the choreographer to make "hoofers" out of the cast of attractive young females who showed up for auditions. Sherry Britton, a burlesque headliner who first started out in the chorus at the People's Theater on the Bowery, remembers, "One of the numbers that we did that was created by our choreographer was [inspired by] the Civil War. They got us uniforms from a costume house, blue and the gray. We marched around, and marched around. And at the end they dropped an enormous American flag, and had us saluting very patriotically, bare-breasted [CHUCKLES]." At the same time, the choreographers worked with the big stars of the circuit, helping them develop their individual styles and perfect their routines that would garner notices and jobs for them from coast to coast. The queens had to have a repertoire of numbers to cull from, changing

Dancer Bernice signed this photo for Paul Morokoff.

OPPOSITE PAGE (TOP):
Athena the Grecian Siren of Sex.

OPPOSITE PAGE (BOTTOM):
Camille 2000.

their acts so the audiences wouldn't get bored.

Girls formed close relationships with their choreographers; if a choreographer took a special interest in a particular girl, it was possible for her to make the transition from an extra to a star in a short time. Professionalism in rehearsals was as important as in legitimate theater; performers had to arrive on time to practice complicated production numbers, talking scenes with the comedians, and solo spots. Discipline and dedication were requirements for success.

Paul Morokoff, a choreographer and producer of burlesque shows, worked with some of the biggest names in burlesque on the East Coast. Coaching chorus girls and headliners such as Lois de Fee, Blaze Starr, and Ann Corio (he choreographed and stage managed Corio's show *This Was Burlesque*), Paul was responsible for helping strippers develop into dancers. He taught rhythm to those who didn't possess it naturally, gave exercise programs to trim hefty waistlines, and addressed the issue of stage fright by teaching his new girls to focus on the timing of the music rather than the audience.

Paul was born in 1904 in Ohio and got his start as a choreographer at the Hollywood Theater in Detroit, where he met chorus boy and future costume designer Rex Huntington. Paul staged the big production numbers of the chorus girls at the Hollywood and helped many of the queens who passed through the theater to refine their routines. In the late 1940s Paul moved to New Jersey, where he became an in-house producer and choreographer at the Hudson Theater in Union City.

Athena the Grecian Siren of Sex, a.k.a. Helen Morrison, who passed away in September 2001, got her start in burlesque after seeing the chorus girls kicking in line at the Hudson. She found the nerve to approach Paul for an audition and became part of the chorus. Athena told me that, as one of Paul's chorus girls, she "did about five or six different numbers and rehearsed every week for the following show for other numbers."

Camille 2000, a.k.a. Camille Sands, a burlesque queen known as "the girl for yesterday, today, and tomorrow," traveled to New York in order to be molded into a star by Paul. Camille told me that it took her years of working with Paul and quite a bit of money spent on wardrobe to evolve into a proper queen. She remembers that Paul stressed to her, "You've got to be slow. And you've got to wear these old-fashioned gowns." Paul died in 1978 in Union City at the age of seventy-three.

Lillian Hunt, a choreographer at the Los Angeles Follies Theater, worked with West Coast queens such as Betty Rowland and Tempest Storm as well as with the Follies chorus girls. Gussie Gross says Lillian was not only responsible for her own start as a costume designer, but was also the Svengali behind Tempest Storm's transformation into a burlesque queen. Gussie says when she first met Tempest, "she was a barmaid at the old Burbank Theater. She used to drink a quart of Scotch every single day. She weighed about a hundred and seventy pounds and when [Lillian Hunt] got a hold of her . . . she put her on a diet and got her off the booze and then she turned out to be fantastic." Lillian created some of her most extravagant acts for Tempest, such as a Venus-inspired routine, in which Tempest emerged "nude" (in a flesh-colored leotard) from a giant seashell and slowly put on her clothes.

Lillian was also responsible for the evolution of Shirley Jean Rickert, child star of the *Little Rascals* series, into a professional burlesque queen. When Shirley Jean went to the Follies Theater to look for work as a chorus girl in between film jobs, Lillian picked her out of the chorus, named her "Gilda and Her Crowning Glory," and proceeded to train her in the art of striptease. Gussie Gross, of course, provided the appropriate attire.

Established mainstream choreographers also drew inspiration from the burlesque world. As a teenager, Bob Fosse got his start as half of the vaudeville dancing team called "The Riff Brothers" and often performed with strippers on the same bill. His fascination with the art of striptease is evident in many of his works, such as *Cabaret, Pippin, Sweet Charity, Damn Yankees,* and *All That Jazz,* which feature strip-motivated numbers. In *Lenny*, a film based on the life story of burlesque comedian Lenny Bruce, Fosse opens with a burlesque striptease set in a nightclub, where Lenny's wife, stripper Hot Honey Harlow, performs to the burlesque standard "Lament," written by Sonny Lester. In the 1939 film *On Your Toes*, even George Balanchine, regarded as the foremost ballet master of the twentieth century, created a dance for ballerina Vera Zorina titled "Slaughter on Tenth Avenue," in which Zorina performs a cleaned up striptease *en pointe*.

Some burlesque queens, such as Betty Rowland, who was trained in ballet as a child, translated their discipline into their striptease, creating a refined or "classy" style. Others were known for their wild, freeform style of dancing, such as Georgia Southern

Joan Torino shakes it. She once told me that she got holes in the crotch of her tights "from too much dancin'."

OPPOSITE PAGE:
Tempest Storm transformed by Lillian Hunt.

who ran around the stage bobbing her head up and down frantically—constantly moving as the layers flew off.

Lili St. Cyr, known for her world-famous bubble bath routine, was considered one of the best dancers in burlesque; other queens admired and respected her grace and flexibility. Burlesque queen Dixie Evans told me that Lili was her number one golden age burlesque queen idol because she "walked like a star, she talked like a star. Her wardrobe, her acts were fabulous . . . flawless." Lois de Fee, a contemporary of Lili's, said that Lili was the "epitome of sexy . . . the way she carried herself . . . when she moved her shoulder. She had all the right [moves]. She moved like a ballet dancer. She was very graceful. And she just oozed sex . . . taking the baths, she made it look like *Wow!*"

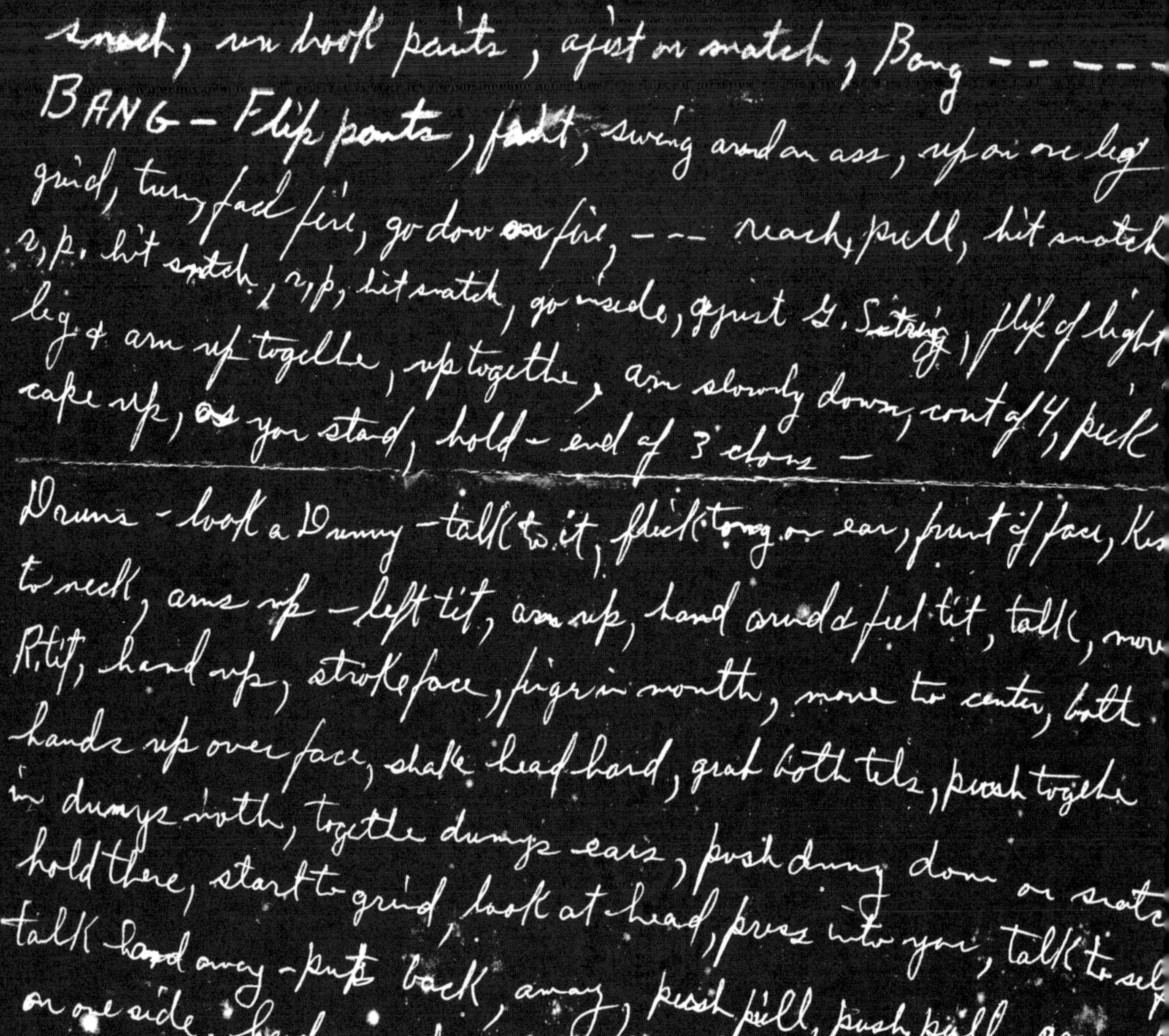

snack, un hook pants, ajust on snatch, Bong - - - -
BANG - Flip pants, fast, swing around on ass, up on one leg
grind, turn face fire, go down on fire, - - reach, pull, hit snatch
2, p. hit snatch, 2, p, hit snatch, go inside, ajust G. String, flik of light
leg & arm up together, up together, arm slowly down, count of 4, pick
cape up, as you stand, hold - end of 3 chorus -

Drums - look a Dummy - talk to it, flick tong on ear, front of face, kiss
to neck, arms up - left tit, arm up, hand around feel tit, talk, move
R. tit, hand up, stroke face, finger in mouth, move to center, both
hands up over face, shake head hard, grab both tits, push togethe
in dumys mouth, togethe dumys ears, push dumy down on snatch
hold there, start to grind, look at head, press into you, talk to self
talk hard away - push back, away, push pull, push pull, arm up
on one side, hand runs down arm slowly, head turns, bite arm,
move lips, sex it up, bump - - - rub stomach, hold breath,
scream, drop dumy, - end of drums -
Love for Sale - 12 bars -

Burlesque queen Zorita's handwritten notations on her choreography.

OPPOSITE PAGE:
Burlesque attracted varied talents, including the usual singers, dancers, and comedians, as well as more unusual acts such as contortionists.

Murray
Korman
N.Y.

BELOW:
October 1957: A burlesque stripper dancing to a solo piano man. The days of the full orchestra were long gone. Dixie Evans recalls, "Nobody could move themselves from the TV. . . . The theaters closed one by one and the musicians dropped off. You had seven men in the pit, you got five, you got four, you got three, you got two. The last time you go around the circuit, there's one little fellow with his glasses hanging on his head, playing the piano, tooting the horn. [Burlesque] was over in the fifties, the middle fifties, it just died, the big theaters closed."

RIGHT:
Patti Waggin in the throes of back-bending ecstasy.

FAR RIGHT:
Carol Pearce poses and struts for photographer Bill Thomas in his Los Angeles studio.

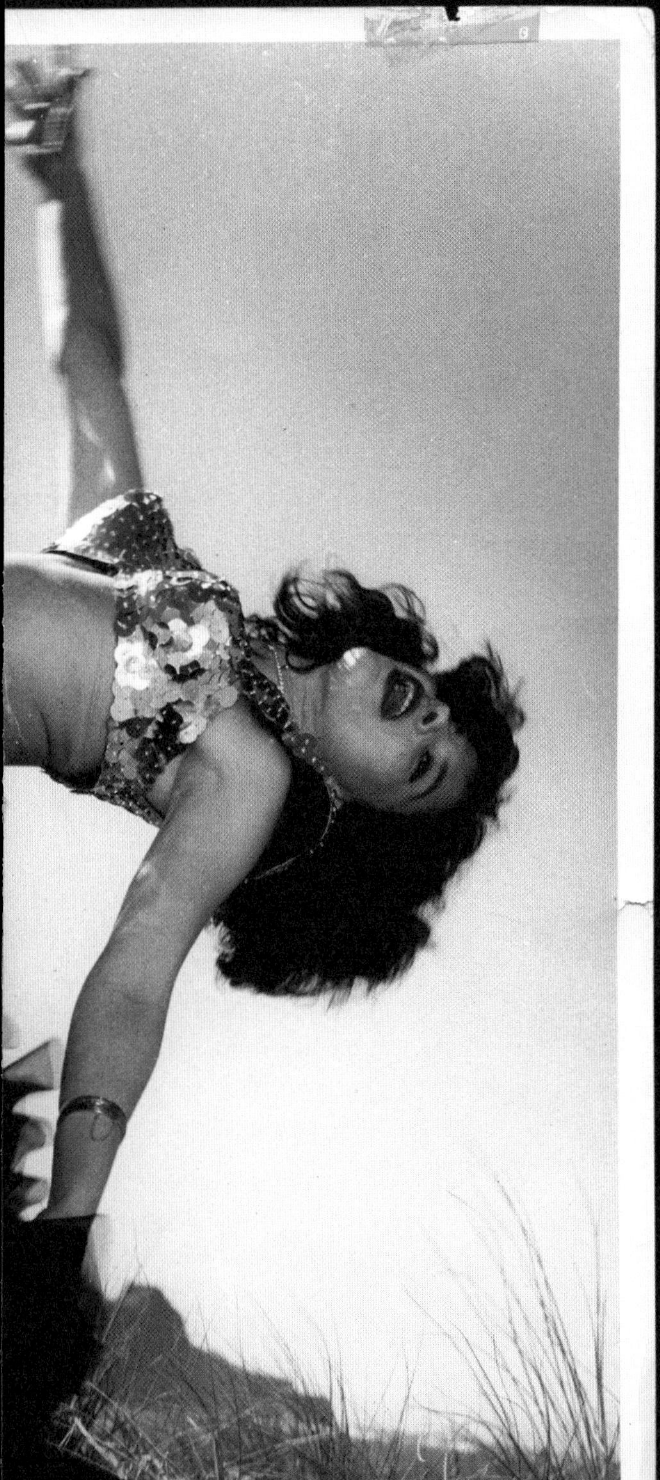

SWINGIN
Lorali, star
the New Fol

Known for her beauty and sumptuous costumes, Exotic Lorali was a graceful dancer and one of Gussie Gross's clients.

is
at
ter.

KODAK SAFETY FILM

Gimmicks

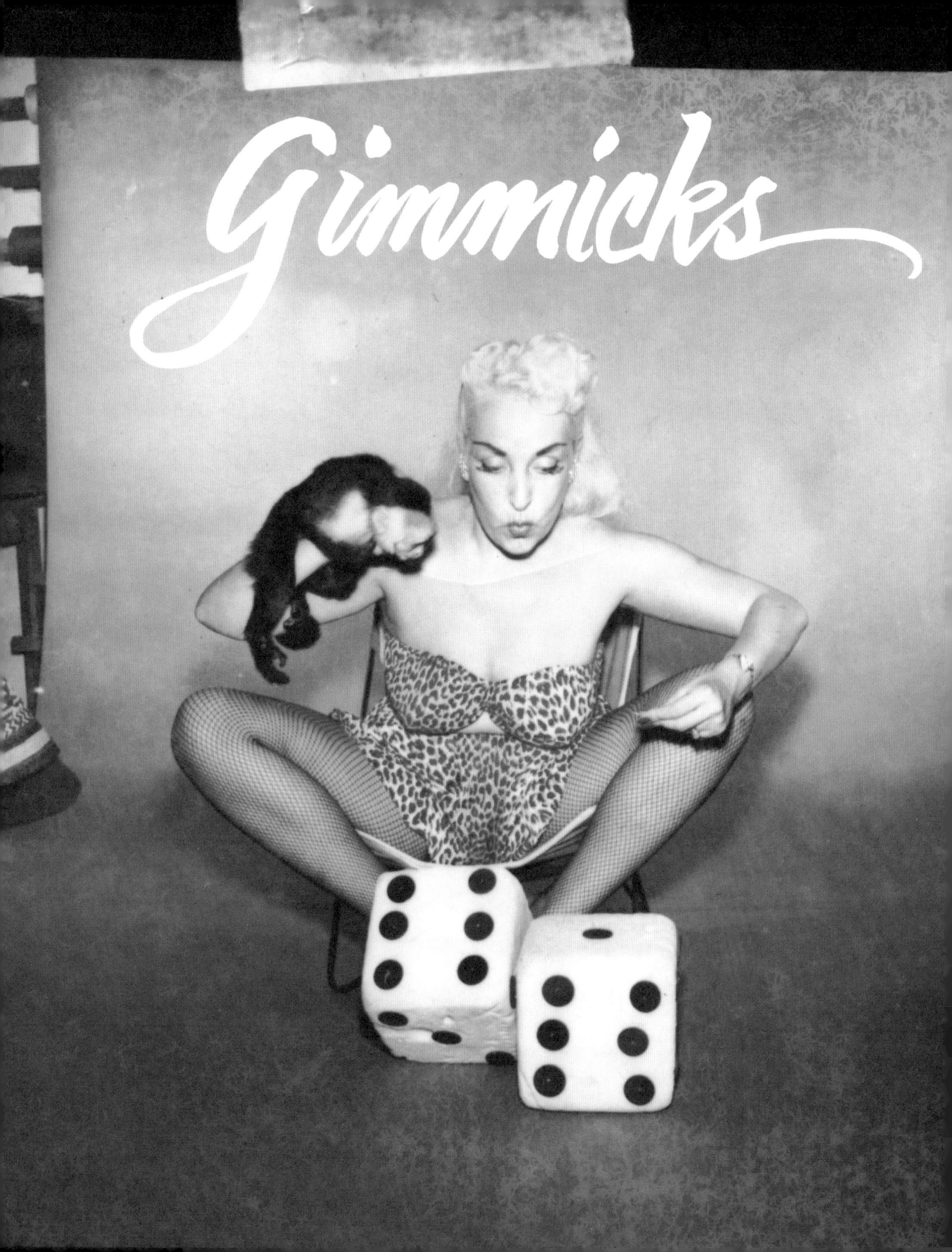

JENNIE LEE
The Bazoom Girl

JENNIE LEE
"*The* BAZOOM GIRL"

In order to make their mark on the burlesque scene as featured stars, potential queens needed to create and refine their own signature "gimmick" or act. Gypsy Rose Lee has often been quoted as saying, "You gotta have a gimmick." Hers was the novelty of being an "intellectual" burlesque queen. According to famed burlesque queen Zorita, Gypsy's and Ann Corio's gimmicks were similar—teasing the audience with the unfulfilled promise of removing clothing. She further explained to me, "Ann Corio's little take off line as she started to strip down was, 'Ooh!!! I can't take that off, I'd catch cold!!' Gypsy did her entire number, very dignified. Everything was done in a form of prose or poetry or song. Gypsy didn't do a typical strip. She did Gypsy. The same as I did Zorita and Sherry did Sherry. Sherry copied a lot of little movements and things—a little hand movement that I did—but they were just ballet movements." Gypsy's mainstream success influenced other queens who learned to identify themselves with a particular act.

Sally Rand accessorized with a giant bubble and feather fans; Lili St. Cyr performed in a simulated bubble bath; Zorita performed with a pair of eight-pound boa constrictors; Rosita Royce danced with live macaws on her shoulders; and Ricky Covette, at six-foot-eight, used her tremendous height as her gimmick and was known as "The World's Tallest Exotic."

There was great competition among the girls and it was not unheard of to copyright an act. Some routines were so popular that queens incorporated them into their repertoires. For example, Gypsy Rose Lee performed a reverse strip—starting out in a corset and ending up fully dressed. Lili St. Cyr liked this idea and made it her own by performing it on a faux backstage set—starting out in her dressing gown and stockings and slowly getting ready to meet a stage door Johnny for a night out in her cocktail attire.

A cartoon take-off on burlesque queen Rosita Royce and her macaws, a popular burlesque act.

OPPOSITE PAGE:
Jennie Lee, "The Bazoom Girl," was known for her spectacular tassel-twirling skills.

PREVIOUS PAGE:
Detail from a contact sheet of Diane and her monkey.

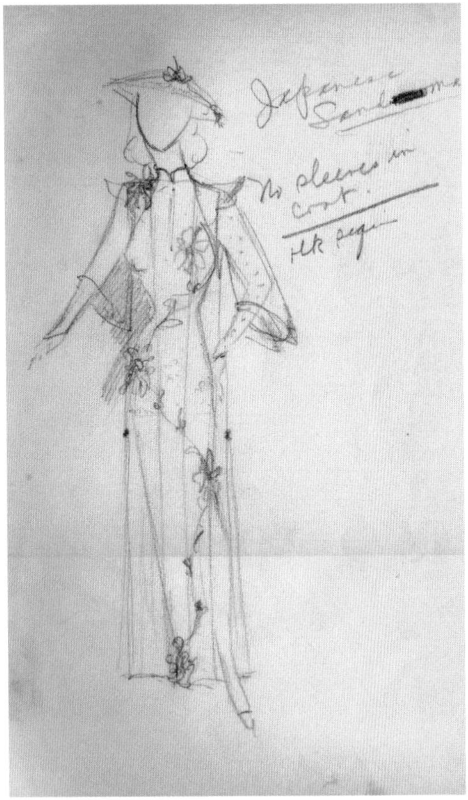

A Japanese sandman costume sketch by Rex Huntington. According to Rex, "It's the gimmick that makes a girl stand out. For instance she may want to look like a huge white bird when she steps out onstage. That's clever because it is different. So I make her a complete outfit from feathers—yes, real maribou or ostrich feathers. Her panties, her bra, her slip, pasties, her baby-doll outfit and shoulder wrap are all made of feathers. It often takes me weeks to finish such a costume, but I've never yet failed a girl."

Dixie Evans, who was known as the "Marilyn Monroe of Burlesque," said, "The competition was horrendous . . . You have to have something terribly unusual to be the star." Dixie and I met in 1997 when we began corresponding about the golden years of burlesque. She runs a museum called Exotic World, started by burlesque queen Jennie Lee, whose gimmick was her large "bazooms." When Jennie passed away, Dixie took over the responsibility of running Exotic World. Though it functions as a museum, Exotic World still pursues the goals of the League of Exotic Dancers by helping out retired burlesque queens, many of whom fell on hard times when their youth and beauty gave way to old age and medical bills. Out in the California desert, Dixie keeps the flames of burlesque burning with stories of stripteasers past. One of the later stars of burlesque, Dixie gained fame in the late forties and fifties with her Marilyn impersonation. Dixie was an invaluable resource for my research, providing me with information and leads to other long-lost burlesque queens. She told me that some of the women had found religion or didn't want to be contacted, preferring to keep their burlesque days in the past.

It was often burlesque theater owners and producers who named queens and gave them a gimmick. Harold Minsky gave Dixie her moniker and gimmick because he thought she resembled Marilyn Monroe. She then had gowns made by costumer Rex Huntington in the style of Marilyn's glamorous wardrobe, and learned to impersonate Marilyn's speaking voice: "I used to come on in curtain one and I'd say [in Marilyn Monroe's voice] 'Well, it just wasn't that easy to become a movie star. I had to walk and walk and knock on every agent's door till I felt I would drop. But, somehow, I just had to reach the top.' And then the set would open up and I walk toward the movie camera and the producer's chair. Of course, Marilyn did try to sue me, which, I don't blame her for, but at the same time, I'm thinking, if she's so famous why is she worried about me? I'm way down here making nothing. She's way up there."

Betty Rowland, known as "The Ball of Fire," says that she was once billed as the "'Tiniest Stripper in Burlesque' . . . I didn't choose that though . . . When I came out to California to perform, one of the brothers who owned the theater [where I was working] saw me dance in the first show. He said 'You're a regular ball of fire.' I thought that was really corny but it stuck."

Dixie Evans' measurements by Rex Huntington.

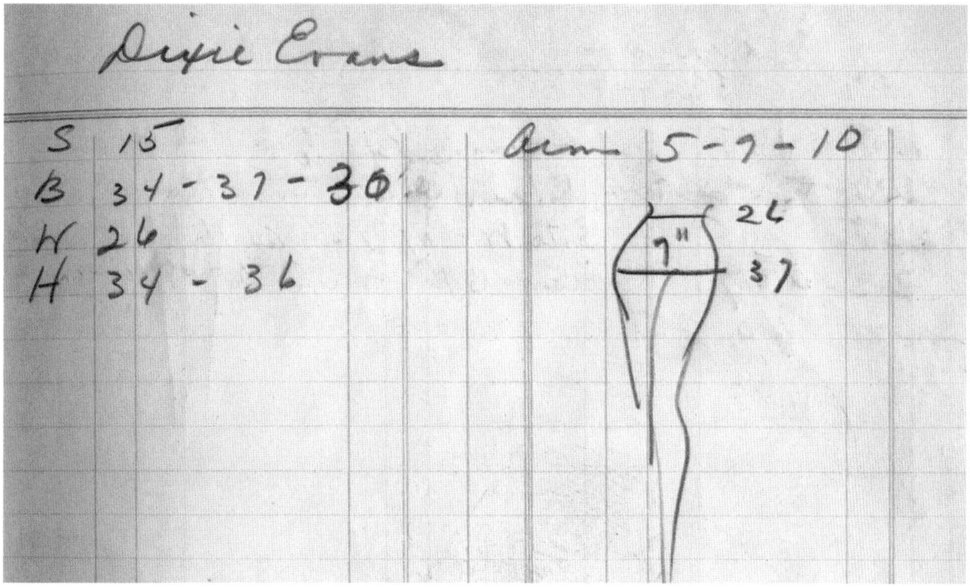

Other queens, such as the bawdy Rose la Rose, were known for their inventive acts, just shy of crossing the line. Leroy Griffiths, a burlesque theater owner and contemporary strip club proprietor, says that Rose "did one number, I called it Sputnik, where she would come out of the ceiling down on a spaceship. And she would land and she was dressed in a spacesuit and she'd walk over to [an audience member] and say, 'What's your name?' He said, 'Johnny.' She said, 'Well, Johnny, did you ever see the Milky Way?' And she'd throw her bra off and there would be the Milky Way. And then she announced, 'How about the moon?' She'd strip off the back of her, there's the moon. She was always doing something that was up to date at that time."

Burlesque costume designers were integral to bringing each queen's gimmick to life. Designers Gussie Gross and Rex Huntington worked with their clients to ascertain their talents and visually develop their gimmicks. For Athena the Grecian Siren of Sex, Rex created Grecian goddess gowns. Gimmicks inspired by the exoticism of foreign lands called for costumes with endless layers of ruffles, multitudes of feathers, and adornment of all types, such as fruit trimmings and bird hats. Gussie made skirts for the dancer Chili

Pepper with tiers of Latin ruffles; for Frenchy Le Vonne, she fashioned "a little French [maid] outfit with garters and all"; and for Tana the Persian Princess, she designed an ornate harem-inspired wardrobe complete with headdresses, capes, and handbeaded gowns.

Clients wrote letters to their costumers while on the road, asking for new pieces to fit their latest gimmick. La Contessa, an Eastern European performer who passed herself off as a countess, sent Gussie numerous notes detailing what she needed: "Say, and say fast . . . I need new costume like black one. Can you make it? But beautiful aqua color or flaming red without fitting bodice. . . . Mine went to pieces. I need another and fast in ten days of time. Let me know at once please and price . . . All my wardrobe rags. See me coming back to LA. At least I need three news ones. My warmest regards, La Contessa."

There were still some queens who felt they didn't need a gimmick, just a strong presence. Athena the Grecian Siren of Sex said that Tempest Storm "didn't have a gimmick. She didn't need one [because] she was a beautiful girl." Lois de Fee, who was six-foot-four, said that if she did have a gimmick in her heyday, it was her height, but she tried to shy away from relying on her physical stature to gain fans. She added, "I had a very elegant white jersey draped dress made . . . and I tried to do it very ladylike. I didn't bump or grind or anything. I did more of a Ziegfeld parade type thing. But the boys liked it."

OPPOSITE PAGE:
A Gussie Gross sketch for her client Chili Pepper, who was known for her arousing dancing.

Examples of Parisian chic executed by Gussie Gross for her client Frenchy.

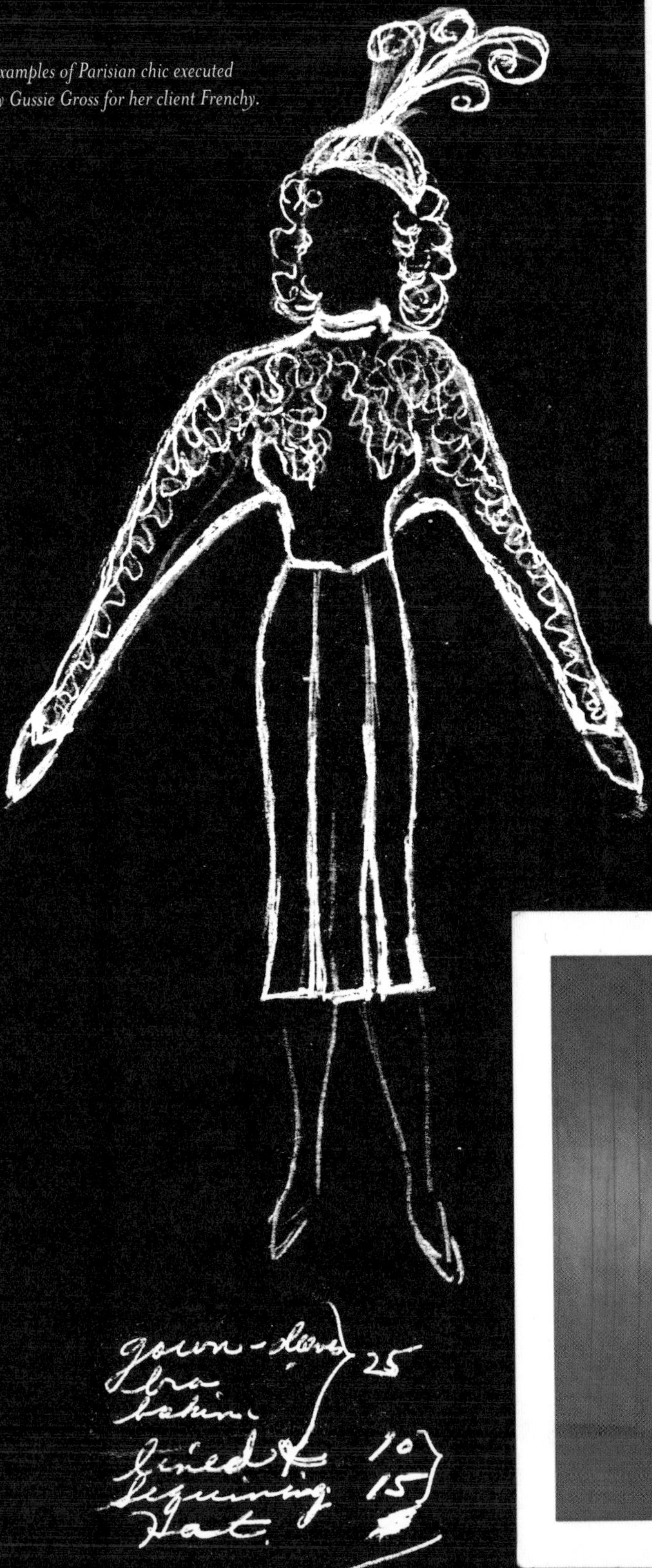

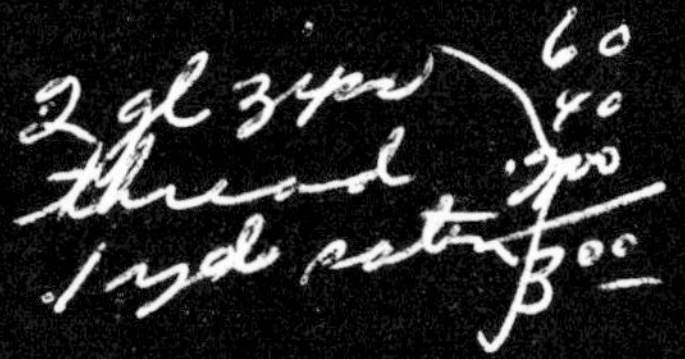

★ ★ "WORLD'S TALLEST EXOTIC!"

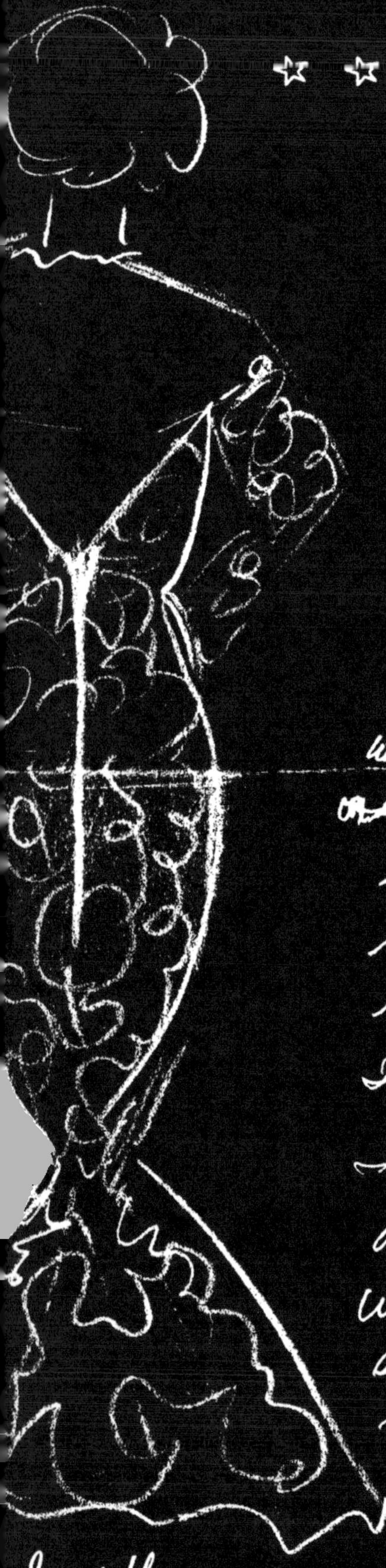

Inimitable

Dear Bussie

I'm just not an artist but this is the general idea.

In black cotton embordiered lace - ~~with~~ nude flesh ~~on top~~ - under the lace use a heavier material so my lace pants won't show through.

The lace here runs about 3.00 a yard. wasn't able to get enough so I hope you can match it. It seems to be standard stock. and about the only one I liked.

Short Story About A Tall Girl

Rickey Covette, 23, does not mea[n to] give men an inferiority complex. [But] she does.

Miss Covette, of Hollywood, Ca[lif.], comes in a "queen-size" package six [feet] eight inches tall. The average m[an] talking to her, feels as if he is stan[ding] in a pit.

Architecturally sound, her meas[ure]ments are 38"—26"—37". She we[ighs] 152 pounds.

Miss Covette is in Detroit for a n[ight] club engagement. She is billed as "[the] world's tallest exotic."

She visited the Free Press Fri[day]. Her height commanded attention.

"I felt very self-conscious about [my] height when I was 14," she said. "[Then] I made up my mind to emphasize it instead of trying to hide it with [flat] shoes."

She feels that she is an advance [model] of the woman of tomorrow.

"The height of the average wo[man] in the last 10 years has increased [two] inches," she said.

"All women will be as tall as I [am] 500 years from now."

A major drawback to such sta[ture], Miss Covette reluctantly admits.

"Big feet."

SS GUSSIE, YOUR GOWN IS A SENSATION! THANKS * LOADS! Ricki

This Was The Biggest Assignment Reporter Charles Manos Had All Day.

"Tana" The Persian Princess

purple
Bra side view
flesh net

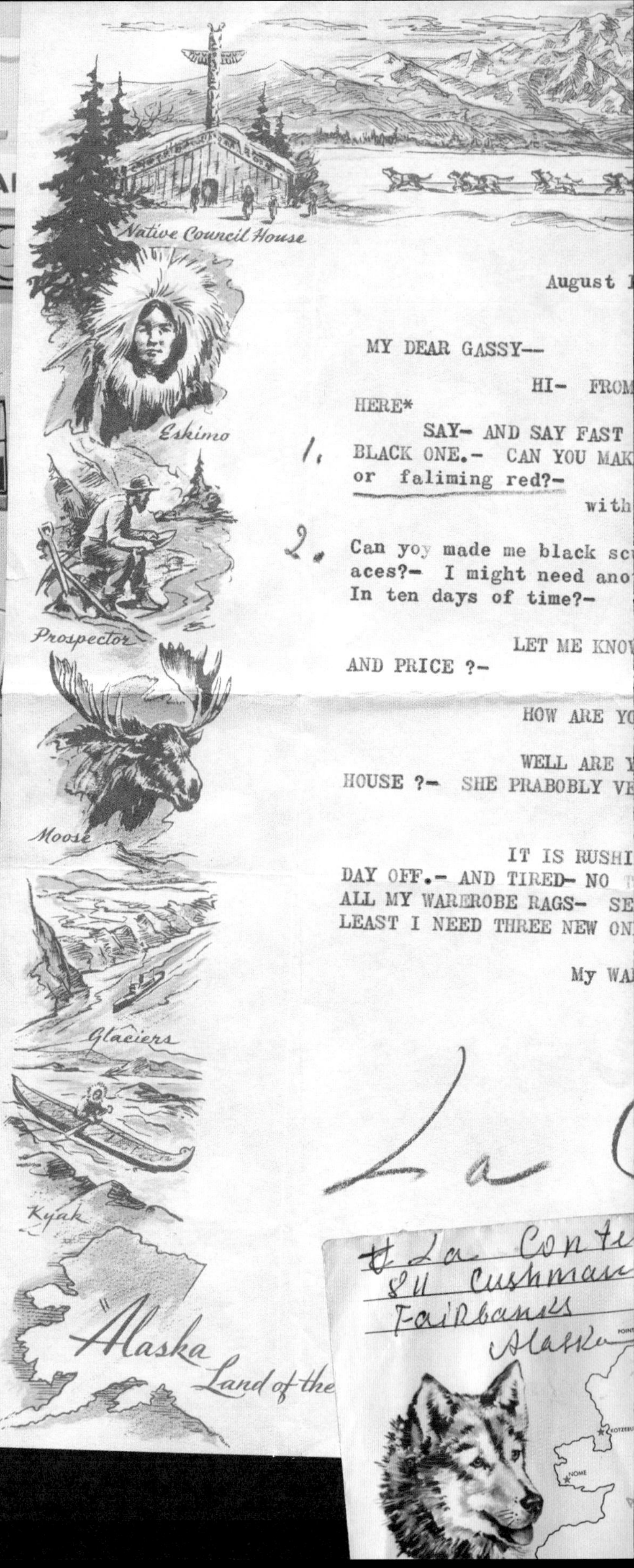

August

MY DEAR GASSY--

HI- FROM
HERE*

SAY- AND SAY FAST
1, BLACK ONE.- CAN YOU MAK
or faliming red?-
with

2, Can yoy made me black sc
aces?- I might need ano
In ten days of time?-

LET ME KNOW
AND PRICE ?-

HOW ARE YO

WELL ARE Y
HOUSE ?- SHE PRABOBLY VE

IT IS RUSHI
DAY OFF.- AND TIRED- NO
ALL MY WAREROBE RAGS- SE
LEAST I NEED THREE NEW ON

My WA

La C

La Conte
811 Cushman
Fairbanks
Alaska

Correspondence and photos sent by La Contessa to Gussie Gross from the road.

~~20-~~
40- 75⁰⁰
5.
30

AM OLREDY THREE MONTH

ED NEW COSTUME LIKE
BEUTIFUL AQUA-COLLAR?

boddise ?-

hat one- My went to pe-
ast.- (Bodice O'K.)

PLEACE.-

RS ?-

OUR LITTLE GIRL OUT OF
AH ?-

AS I WORKING WITHOUT
YTHING.-
NG BACK TO L.A. At

RDS.
LA CONTESSA

ntessa

AIR MAIL

Mrs. Gussie Gross
3061 Lanfranco St.

 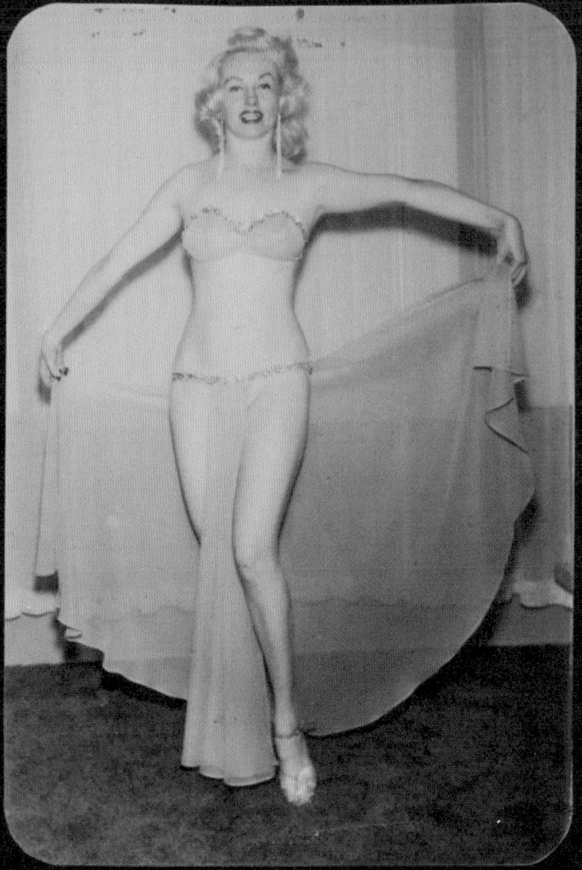

put, a few ruffels of
net (any color) under neith
like a ballerena - make
net on a seperate band and
tack it under, so when
I have it cleaned I can
detatch net,

Dixie sums up best where most of the stars of the burlesque scene ended their careers with this anecdote about her failed marriage: "I did marry a prize fighter . . . professional prize fighter, he helped me a lot but he would never carry my luggage. He said, 'What will people think if I carry your luggage?' And we got along very good. A prize fighter at the end of his career is something like probably a stripper at the end of her career, not quite so glamorous."

OPPOSITE PAGE:
This sketch, which Dixie enclosed in a note to Gussie Gross, illustrates the collaborative nature of the client/costume designer relationship.

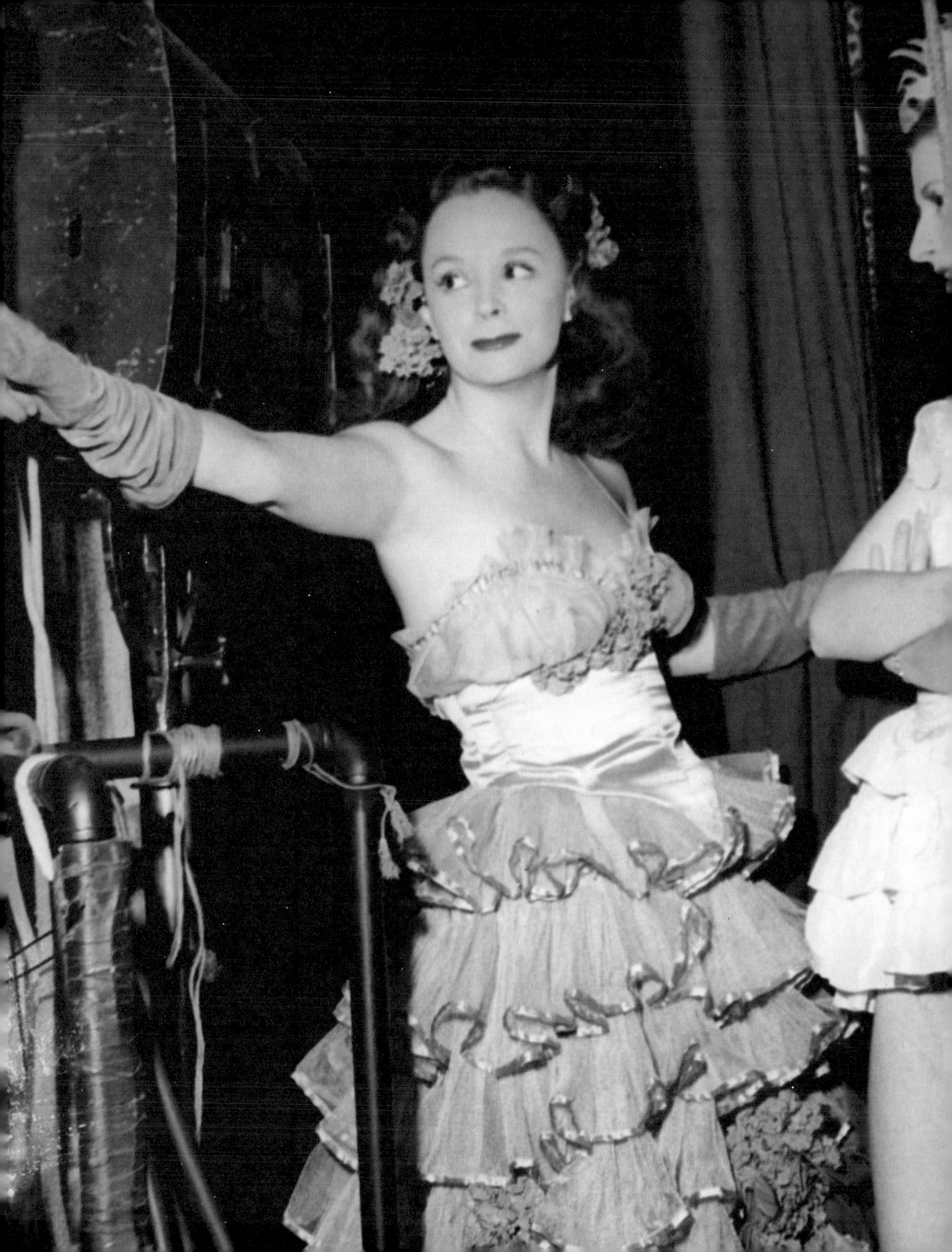

Backstage

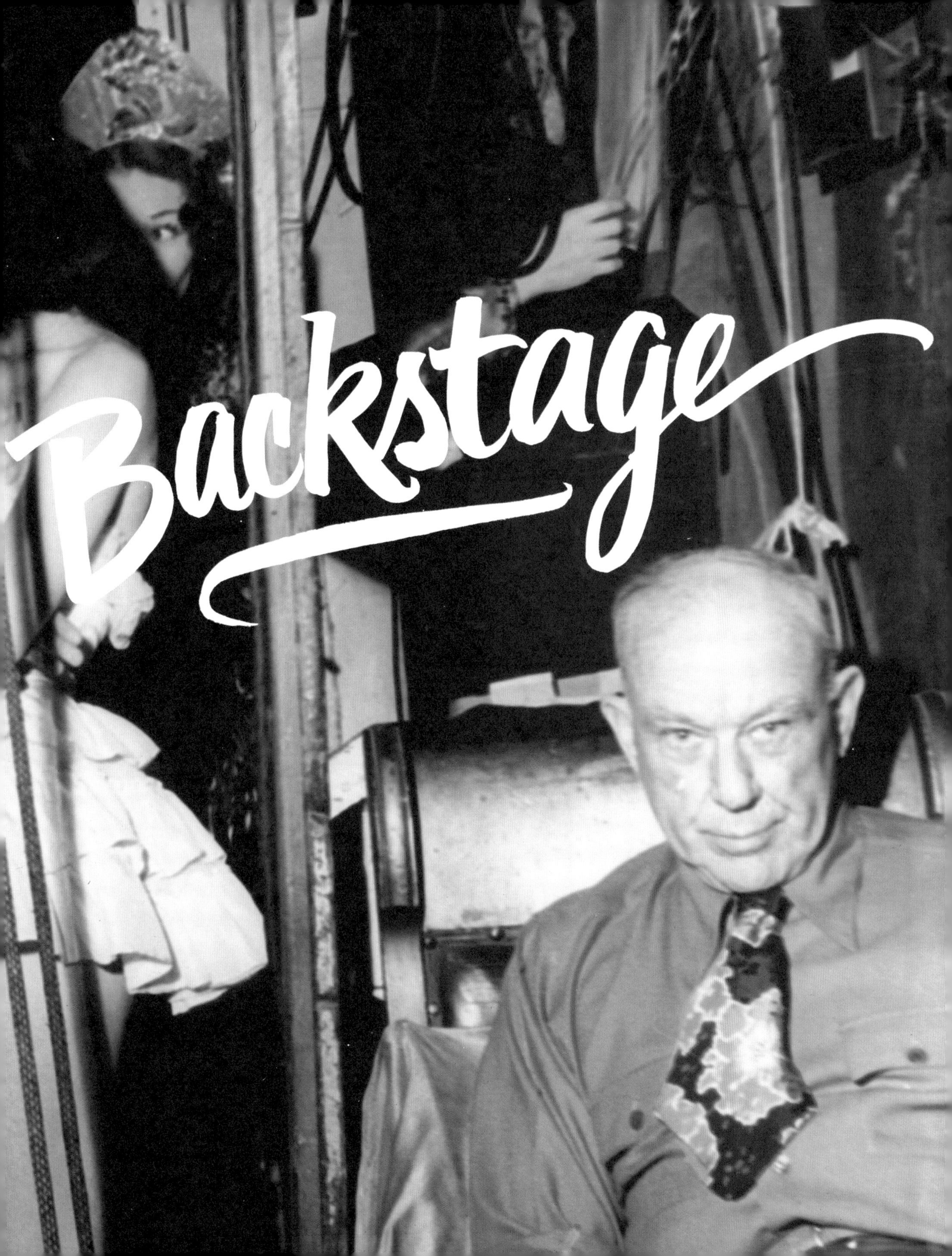

The backstage of a burlesque theater served as the innermost sanctum of the burlesque queen's world. Stage managers closely guarded the entrance to the backstage area, ensuring that no unwanted guests or stage door Johnnies breached the security of the private dressing rooms. Burlesque queens constantly received fan letters and flowers sent backstage from admirers hoping to take them out; after all, having an incredible icon of femininity on one's arm proved a man's status and prowess.

Women rested between shows in the dressing rooms, gossiping about their lives and trading costume ideas and makeup tips. Sherry Britton said that she first learned about pasties from another stripper in the dressing room: "In 1951, I came back from Europe and I didn't know what to do with my life, so I decided to go back into burlesque. I got a job at the Rialto Theatre in Chicago. I went backstage, and I saw that people were wearing pasties. So I said, 'Where do you get pasties?' And they said, 'Ask that blonde girl over there.' And I did. I said, 'Where do I get pasties?' And she looked at me and said, 'What size are the knockers, kid?'"

Betty Rowland checks her feathers before leaving her dressing room.

OPPOSITE PAGE:
A dancer at her dressing table mugs for the camera.

The chorus girls shared a dressing area while the stars got their own rooms, though it was generally not a fancy step up. Nonetheless, the queens personalized their rooms with knickknacks and tried to make them their home away from home. Zorita recalls,

> Most of the dressing rooms were pigpens. I had sheets with hooks that would completely cover my dressing room and my walls. I [usually chose sheets in] pink because I found pink more flattering to your face. I would send the head of the backstage a twenty dollar bill and say, please give my dressing room a coat of paint because I didn't want to follow some girl

> in and look at filthy walls. You didn't have your own toilet. You had to use [communal] toilets, which didn't amuse me at all . . . usually I wound up peeing in the sink. [I] had a chair cover that had pockets in it . . . there were two pockets in the back . . . your brassiere went in one pocket and G-strings went in another pocket . . . and there were four pockets for your shoes. [I] didn't put my bottom down on a filthy chair that somebody else had had their bottom on. [I] tried to make [my] dressing room as comfortable and livable as possible because [I] was going to put so many hours in there.

Zorita was extremely ornery when her dressing room didn't live up to her standards. In one incident in Baltimore, she came to blows with a theater owner, Hans Nickels, who wouldn't put a fresh coat of paint on her walls and toilet. Apparently, he told her that it was bad luck to paint anything in the theater once the season started. Zorita called Hans "a Nazi" and decided to craft her revenge. She said, "I came out in the finale of the show . . . with a big cape, and just when the curtain was closing, I dropped my cape, stood there, and shook my ass with a big swastika on my ass."

Though it may seem that Zorita was overly fastidious about the cleanliness of her dwellings, it wasn't unjustified. Like many other queens who traveled with family members who waited backstage during performances, Zorita traveled with her young daughter. She said that she "had a dresser drawer [in my room] and I had a big pillow in the dresser drawer, [and I] put my kid on the pillow in the dresser drawer. [I] went down, did my number and then came back up and I could take her to work with me."

Queens also socialized with their friends backstage, if they happened to be on the same bill. Sherry and Zorita first met in 1936, backstage at a theater in San Francisco where they were both slotted to perform. Zorita, an out lesbian, told me that she "banged that broad [Sherry] on the dressing room floor—she liked it and stuck around for more."

Sherry tells the story differently. She says that she and Zorita "had connecting dressing rooms. [The door between us] had a top and a bottom. While I was putting my things away the top opened, and Zorita [gave me an appraising look] and said, 'We're going to get along fine.' I said, 'Excuse me,' and closed the door because I was naked . . . It

OPPOSITE PAGE:
Sue Martin hams it up backstage.

sounds kind of naïve or childish, but I was still kind of modest. Two seconds later she came through the other door of my dressing room, threw this enormous mink coat on the floor, threw me on it, and proceeded to part my legs and tried to make love to me. And I looked at her—I couldn't believe what was happening. I said, 'Excuse me!' [CHUCKLES] And I got up and opened the door and threw the coat out. And she came after it. And we managed to become friends, but always platonic."

In addition to all the codes of conduct backstage, it was a big taboo to watch other strippers' acts from the wings. It was acceptable to watch the sketches or production numbers, but the burlesque queens did not allow a side audience because they were concerned that other strippers might copy their routines and they didn't like the distraction. Lois de Fee told me that it was "dog eat dog. You had to stay on your toes to keep your spot." When I asked her if many strippers copied each others' acts, she said, "Oh sure. Lili St. Cyr's own sister Dardy Orlando took her whole act verbatim. That's when they stopped speaking." Sherry told me, "If you were caught watching in the wings you got a bloody nose."

More than one queen expressed distaste for comedian Jerry Lewis's backstage behavior and blatant disregard for this cardinal rule. Jerry's father Danny Lewis was a burlesque performer, and traveled with young Jerry in tow. Betty Rowland said, "[Jerry] would be in the dressing rooms and all over the place and it was most annoying. He'd come in your dressing room and say [about the naked girls] 'Oh, I like that.' And his dad would be saying, 'Jerrrryyyy, let's go.' [Jerry] loved being in the wings watching, as we'd go on, which is taboo for strippers who don't like that. It distracts because you've got to do your act and [you don't want] somebody there talking to you. It's not exactly kosher."

Improprieties aside, backstage life apparently left an impression on the children of the performers and theater owners. Sid Michaels, whose father owned the Old Howard—a famous burlesque theater in Boston—told me that he hung around the backstage areas at five and six years old and that he thought the strippers "were just ladies." Athena the Grecian Siren of Sex, who brought her two children on the road with her, said that the kids loved to watch her act from the wings because they thought "their mommy was a star."

Lillian Hunt, choreographer for such stars as Tempest Storm, Patti Waggin, Lily Ayers, and Gilda poses with Leon DeVoe, stage director and actor.

The peppery chorus cuties pause between numbers. Penny Cillin and Patricia in front. Dixie Christy and Joy Rider in back.

Slats Taylor wants his shirt back but Harry Clexx protests? Penny and Pat.

Joy Rider admires her leading man Bill London, actor deluxe who doubles as comedian.

Novita receiving the fatherly blessing.

The backstage cut up and all-around New Follies favorite Penny Cillin.

Sexy lineup confronts "nosey" Leon DeVoe, who prepares for attack on Penny, Joy and Dixie.

A top photog meets a top entertainer. Our Bill Thomas and Patti Waggin.

(Photos by Bill Thomas)

tissues

KLEENEX

PREVIOUS PAGE:
Betty Rowland drinks tea backstage with fellow performers.

OPPOSITE PAGE:
Betty backstage in her dressing room at Minsky's.

THIS PAGE:
Betty backstage at the Body Shop on the Sunset Strip.

Betty recalls, "We had a man at the entrance to backstage and nobody would be back there unless they were allowed or knew somebody in the show . . . We did four [shows] a day, three on Saturday . . . seven days a week. We were kind of tired all day long trying to turn the husbands on." She preferred to write poetry and read books when she had time backstage.

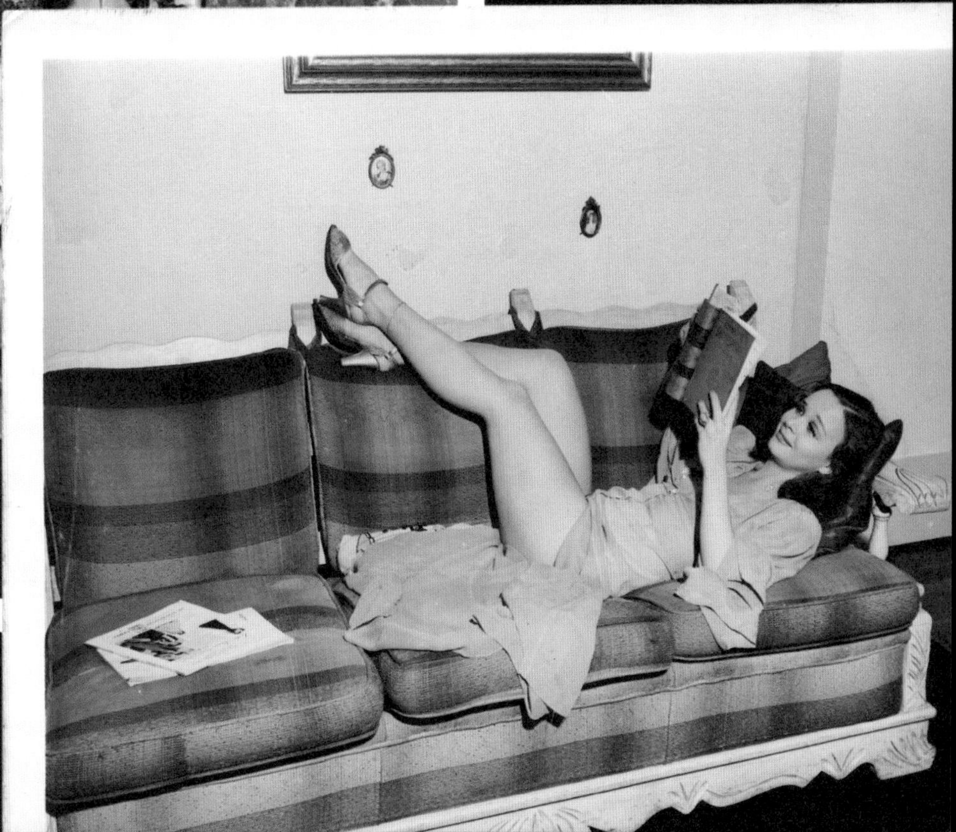

OPPOSITE PAGE: *Dian Rowland and fellow peeler sit on a burlesque comedian's lap.*

BELOW: *Dian poses playfully behind the stage curtain.*

Frenchie, one of Rex Huntington's clients, backstage.

Part II:
The Queens

Betty Rowland

"The Ball of Fire"

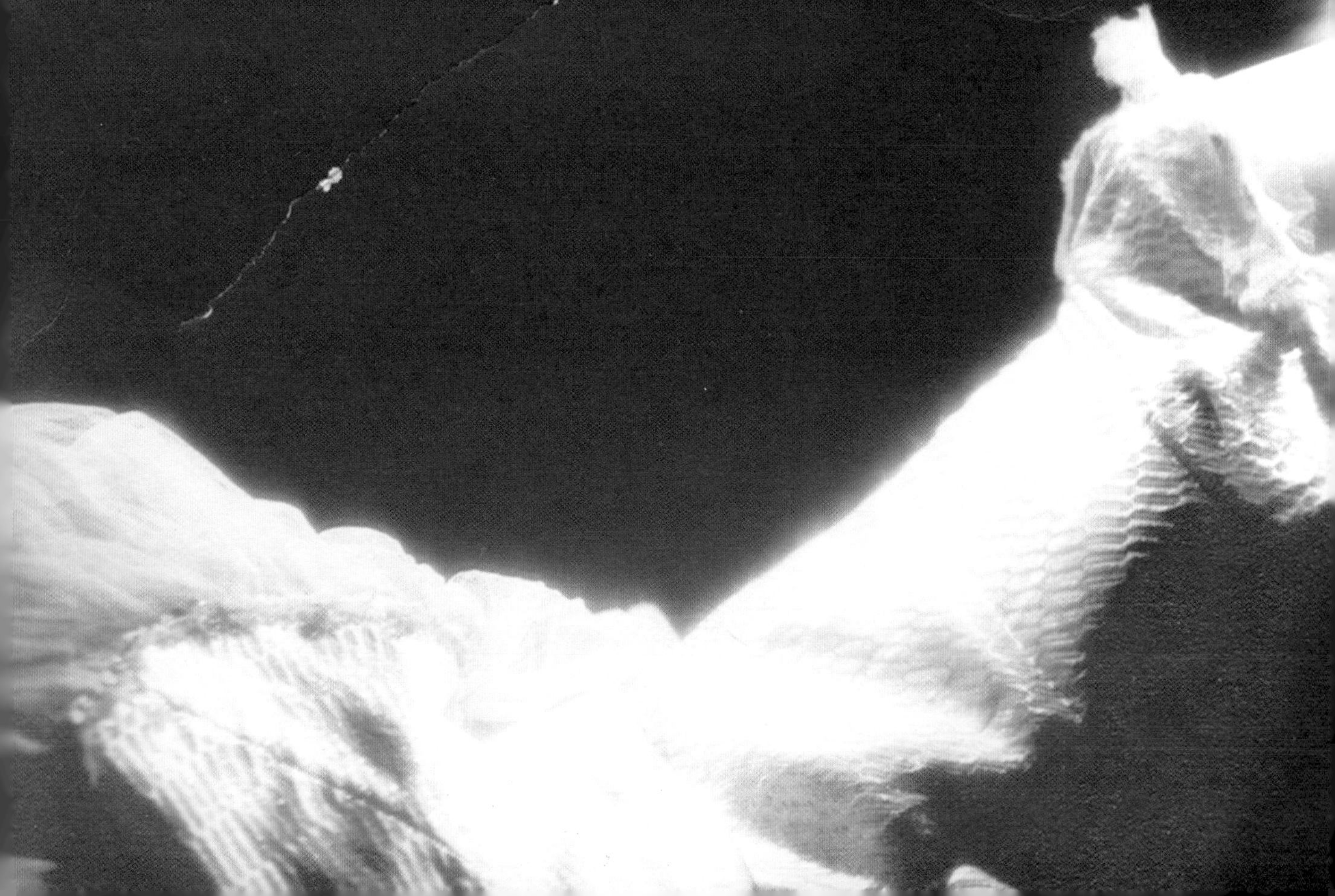

Betty Rowland was the first burlesque queen I met in person. Betty lives in Los Angeles, not far from the house where I grew up. The first time we met, she told me I looked like my grandfather. I wondered how my grandfather, a movie producer of "quality films," had crossed paths with Betty, a famous burlesque queen. In my grandfather's heyday, burlesque was popular entertainment, part of the public lexicon, akin to vaudeville and silent movies.

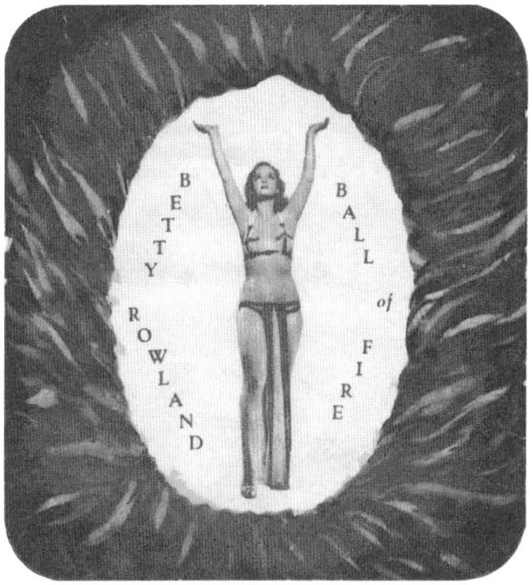

A nightclub coaster advertising Betty as the "Ball of Fire."

Betty explained how they had crossed paths with a lengthy tale that caught me off guard. As a publicity stunt, she sued my grandfather in the 1940s for using her moniker for the title of his film, *Ball of Fire*. Betty had earned the nickname, "Ball of Fire," in the late 1930s during her bump and grind days for her flaming red hair and rhythmic movements. The Samuel Goldwyn picture starred Gary Cooper as an absentminded professor and Barbara Stanwyck as a nightclub singer with a knack for streetwise vernacular. Initially, however, it was intended that Stanwyck's character was to be a burlesque stripteaser.

In screenwriter Billy Wilder's treatment for *Ball of Fire*, I found the original description of Stanwyck's character:" . . . he walks along West 42nd. He stops to look at the billing in front of Minsky's Burlesque. Miss 'Babe' LaBranche, 'The Blonde Blitzkrieg,' is featured in her own rendition of the bubble dance, 'Sexy Suds.' Before he realizes it, he has been steered inside by the ticket-seller and ushered to a seat directly under the runway, which comes out over the audience. When 'Babe' appears, he is overwhelmed both by her devastating misuse of the English language and by her total disregard for the conventional use of clothing."

The Hays commission (known then as the Production Code Administration, or PCA) nixed Wilder's plan and Stanwyck's character

became somewhat gentrified in the process. It was deemed inconceivable that an audience could relate to a woman who took her clothes off for a living. Clearly, the contemporary conception of a burlesque queen was of a "loose" and uneducated woman, and polite society was certainly not ready to accept a burlesque queen as a leading lady.

For this reason, the PCA's censorship cuts to the script alone were quite detailed. In a letter to Samuel Goldwyn dated August 21, 1941, the PCA suggested the following changes: "In the material so far submitted, we note a number of items . . . which seem to be overly sex suggestive . . . and also highly dangerous from the standpoint of official censorship everywhere. Page 75: We note that two or three times throughout the script you use the word 'stripper.' Inasmuch as we cannot, of course, under the Code, approve a 'strip tease,' we suggest therefore that you change this expression." By the time director Howard Hawks began filming, Miss "Babe" LaBranche had become a dancer in a nightclub and her name had been changed to "Sugarpuss O'Shea."

Sugarpuss wears a particularly fetching costume to perform her "Drum Boogie" number. Designed by Paramount costume designer Edith Head, this spectacular outfit of white crepe de chine and sequined paillettes featured a belly-baring jacket and fringed-to-the-thigh long skirt, showing off Barbara's athletic long legs to perfection. Fifty-odd years later, the real "Ball of Fire," Betty Rowland, explained to me that Barbara Stanwyck's costume was a copy of her own self-designed stage attire.

At least a year prior to thc film's release, Betty was headlining at a downtown Los Angeles burlesque theater, the Follies, when Edith Head came in to see her show. Edith came backstage after Betty's set to check out the famed burlesque queen's wardrobe. One particular piece interested her: a floor length cream silk crepe and sequined paneled skirt with a matching long-sleeved cropped blouse. The skirt was slit up to the hip with a series of fringed panels, and both the skirt and blouse unhooked at the sides with large brass hooks and eyes—easy on the fingers but requiring the skill of a professional to remove gracefully. Despite her lawsuit, Betty said that the blatant copy was flattering; having the famous studio designer look to Betty for her fashion sense was a signal that she had "arrived."

Eventually Betty's lawsuit was dropped for lack of evidence. In Howard Hawks' deposition, he mentioned going to the theater with my grandfather and grandmother to see Betty perform. Whether the studio stole her stage character or Betty benefited from the free publicity, the truth remains clouded by perspective and the passing of time. The story binds Betty and me together, however loosely, with memories of a glamorous time filled with once-mythic figures.

Betty was born in Columbus, Ohio, in 1916. Her father did police work and her mother was a housewife. Betty and her three other sisters, Dian, Lorraine, and Rozell, were schooled by their parents to be "good girls," ladylike and well mannered. They got their first taste of show business when their father took the family to Keith's Theatre in Columbus to see a circus revue. Betty and her sisters sat in a box seat and particularly admired a performance by midgets. Betty told her parents that she wanted to be a midget when she grew up.

Her father decided the girls needed to look like "little ladies," so he sent them to dancing school. The Depression had just hit and the girls soon decided to make a little extra money for the family by turning pro. Betty and Rozell started working amateur shows as a sister act in Detroit, where their father had been transferred. About ten years old, in spotless fancy dresses sewn by their mother, they performed a little soft-shoe routine in time to live music—they were the picture of innocence. Their father made them a wooden makeup kit with a mirror inside to take on the road. All in all, it was a family affair, providing good clean entertainment in the vaudeville houses of the day.

From the 1900s to the 1930s in America, burlesque and vaudeville were run on circuits called "wheels." They varied in size and scale. Some, known as "big wheels," were grander and played at theaters in metropolitan areas across the United States; others catered to small-town audiences. For twenty-five cents, one could see an afternoon or evening of entertainment and escape the heat and dreariness of the workday in a dark theater. Burlesque queen Lois de Fee explains, "The big circuit is where I worked . . . the smaller circuit, which I never worked, were the seedier places. They were smaller and cheaply run. They were in small towns. Of course, the people that worked them will hate me for saying it, but it's true: they were more scratch houses—they booked cheaper acts. I mean, they couldn't afford the Ann Corios or the Lois de Fees or the Betty Rowlands or the Zoritas. Maybe that's why they call it scratch house, because it's scratching for money [LAUGHS]."

Betty and Rozell Rowland pose back-to-back.

OPPOSITE PAGE:
A young and innocent Betty.

Both vaudeville and burlesque were similar in format at the turn of the twentieth century, for striptease was not introduced to American burlesque until the early 1920s. Both would have an opening act, orchestra, singers, dancers, comedians, and the grand finale. But apart from this basic lineup, the two types of entertainment couldn't be more different. Vaudeville was pure family entertainment—there were even signs backstage warning the performers not to say "hell" or "damn" in their acts. Burlesque jokes, on the other hand, were suggestive and full of double entendres, often laced with references to bawdy humor. Occasionally one would hear profanity.

When movies became part of the burgeoning entertainment industry, silent films were just one of many acts during a vaudeville show. Soon, however, they began to supplant traditional vaudeville as the preferred form of family entertainment and live performance began to be transferred to celluloid. Many vaudeville actors, including W.C. Fields, made the transition to the big screen, whereas burlesque talent was left mostly untapped due to their provocative nature. The Depression secured the dominance of "talking pictures" as popular escapism, and the vaudeville era was phased out. The Orpheum in downtown Los Angeles was one of the last theaters in America to host two-a-day vaudeville shows. It closed in the mid-1940s.

In the 1930s, the burlesque circuit risked being shut down, as the raunchiness of its shows provoked continual police raids on the theaters. In an effort to clean things up, burlesque shows incorporated tamer vaudeville acts, which often involved sibling acts, usually composed of unrelated, yet attractive young girls billed as "sisters." Thus, when Betty and Rozell left their small town circuit to travel on the "big wheel" in 1933, the Howard Theater in Boston booked their sister act as filler between burlesque shows.

The girls had never seen a striptease and because they performed during breaks between burlesque routines, it was a while before they met their first live stripper. Betty said the first stripteaser she saw was Ann Corio, who was sitting downstairs outside her dressing room, sewing a costume. The girls decided to watch her act, but found it to be mostly "just parading along," not the bumps and grinds they had expected. The next act they caught, Hinda Wasa, was a different story. Betty says they "felt sorry for her, 'cause she wasn't dancing, as far as we were concerned."

Betty and Rozell hadn't told their parents that they were now performing in burlesque theaters rather than vaudeville houses. Eventually their mother got worried and went east to check on the girls. When Mrs. Rowland saw the show, she was shocked and wanted them to quit. But after she went backstage and met all the performers, she realized that Betty and Rozell were keeping no more salacious company than in their vaudeville days.

Soon enough one of the performers wasn't able to do her number, the first strip in the show, and Betty was picked out of the chorus to replace her. (The first strip in a burlesque show was generally given to someone just starting out, while the finale was reserved for the headlining stripteaser.) Betty went out dancing and became so engrossed in the music that she forgot to take her clothes off. She says, "I remember my one sister standing in the wings, and she's saying, why don't we take off a jacket? I was more interested in music . . . [The audience] all thought I was teasing and I really wasn't." Betty adds that she didn't have much trouble succeeding in the beginning spot because "the audience knew you were just starting out" and usually encouraged new acts.

Betty called upon her ballet training to overcome nervousness about performing her first striptease. She said she was so focused on the timing of the music and the cues to remove her clothing in coordination with her dancing that she didn't have time to worry about being nearly nude in front of an audience. Her career took off and she became known as a "classy" burlesque star who integrated ballet moves and striptease in her "bumps in the ballet" routine. She would come on the stage and say to the audience, "Let's put a little juice in the Ballets russes . . . and give the dying swan a little goose—I was always more in tune with Minsky than Nijinsky."

Eventually, Betty's sister, Rozell, also took the place of a stripper who called in sick. The number required that she dance in nothing but silver paint. Her reception was so positive that she changed the silver to gold and earned the moniker "The Golden Girl."

Dian Rowland, a platinum blonde bombshell, became a burlesque queen, too. Sadly, Dian died alone on the road while she was working at a theater in Detroit. When she didn't show up for her spot one night, someone went to check on her and found her dead in her hotel room. The coroner report stated the cause of death to be a heart attack.

Advertising card for the Follies Theater where Sam Goldwyn, Howard Hawks, and Edith Head caught Betty's act.

On tour in London, Rozell Rowland caught the eye of the Baron Empain, who married her in 1936 and took her to live in his chateau Bouffemont outside of Paris, leaving Betty behind in "burley-que." Betty met up with famous burlesque comic Gus Schilling and they became lovers. At the time of her lawsuit with the Samuel Goldwyn Company, Schilling was identified in the deposition as "Mrs. Rowland's husband." Upon reading the deposition myself, I was surprised at the news—Betty had never mentioned this early marriage to me. She since explained that, at that time, the only "polite" way to refer to this type of living arrangement was to call it a "marriage."

Betty says she never thought of burlesque striptease as purely sexual because she was too focused on the technical aspects of her act. When I asked if she felt sexy while she was stripping for an audience, Betty replied that she "hadn't even thought of it—as being what I found out it really was. What you were selling. And in those days it was not that way anyway. It was tease. Tease. We teased . . . that was the name of the game."

I know I don't need to watch my words around Betty; after thirty years in burlesque she must have heard it all. But somehow I feel that talking about—or even acknowledging—the potent sexual fantasy that she provided countless admirers would be beside the point. She exuded such confidence and class. Betty said she never considered herself a "sex object," but rather a dancer and a performer, more akin to an actor in the theater than the topless dancers of today.

Betty's reputation suffered due to her profession. Men thought she would be easy, and women often accused her of being with their husbands. She laughs at the thought that she would ever want to steal anyone's husband, especially those that came to sit in the dark and fantasize about her onstage.

When I asked Betty if she thinks of herself as an inspiration, she answered, "You become a fantasy to other people. Well, that's—it's gratifying. What their gratification is—well that's not my problem . . . But people whisper, for heavens sake, they say, 'Do you know what she used to do?' And they're saying it like I was a porno worker or something. Well they shouldn't whisper—I was a dancer. It was the only thing I knew how to do, and I was a success at it."

Other than Gussie Gross, who designed Betty's costumes in the late 1940s and 50s, Betty sees few of the people she knew from her burlesque days. She doesn't want any part of the current fad for the reunions and reminiscing that several retired burlesquers have started. She separates herself from the later burlesque queens who started stripping in the 1950s by saying, "There's a bunch of [taxi] cab drivers who thought they were limousines."

One day, Betty decided to give me my first striptease lesson. She took me to her closet of costumes, musty and unattended for many years, and chose a gown for me to try on. Suddenly, I felt like a little girl playing dress up. For the first time, I really understood that the clothes and the stance are only part of the burlesque character. I didn't feel the confidence and sexuality that Betty seemed to radiate. I couldn't imagine ever having the guts even to play at taking off my costume, let alone dance in front of an audience at the same time. When I started my research into the world of the great burlesque queens, I fooled myself into thinking that I was simply mesmerized by their wardrobes—but really, it was their attitude and sex appeal that I coveted. I realize now that what I perceived to be "glamour" was something that Betty felt only in small doses—from her costumes, perhaps. Her reality was more complicated than I had imagined.

Holding onto my romantic vision of Betty, I kept pressing her to describe for me just one moment of glamour. After much thought, Betty answered, "Well, there's that moment when the curtains open and there's all those pretty things onstage all dressed up and that's a moment of glamour. And the rest of it, well you can have it."

THIS PAGE AND OPPOSITE :
Gussie Gross took these photos of Betty poolside at Betty's home on Tiger Tail Road in Brentwood, CA.

Watch for
"BALL OF FIRE"
At Your Local Theatre
Coming Soon!

"I love those hick shirts he wears with the boiled collar and the way he always has his vest buttoned wrong...I love him because he's the kind that gets drunk on a glass of buttermilk...I love the way he blushes right up over his ears... *I love him because he don't know how to kiss, the jerk!*"

SAMUEL GOLDWYN, master producer, has scored again! Authors Charles Brackett and Billy Wilder have written a screen play that is both heart warming and uproariously funny—the story of a sedate professor (Gary Cooper) who knew all about dead languages and nothing about live ladies until a night club gal (Barbara Stanwyck) crashed his bachelor quarters and rhumbaed right into his heart.

Under the flawless direction of Howard Hawks, one of the finest casts ever assembled for a Samuel Goldwyn picture hits a laugh-a-minute pace that will give your face a permanent smile and win salvos of applause from critics and public alike.

Gary's serious! *Barbara's delirious!* *Together they're hilarious!*

Samuel Goldwyn presents

GARY COOPER · BARBARA STANWYCK

in

Ball of Fire

Directed by **HOWARD HAWKS**

Photography by Gregg Toland, A.S.C.

Released through RKO Radio Pictures In

OPPOSITE PAGE:
This is the costume Edith Head "referenced" for Barbara Stanwyck in Ball of Fire. *Note the similarity of Head's design to Betty's costume—burlesque queen attire slightly cleaned up for the censors.*

The Rowland Sisters become headliners.

GAIETY
BWAY'S ONLY CONTINUOUS
GIRLIE STAGE SHOW
IRMA VOGELEE ANNETTE
DIAN ROWLAND
Square
ORIGINATIONS
GAIETY FOLLIES
FASTEST GIRLIE SHOWS
Benedict's

Cocktails
twist of lemon peel
CINZANO
VERMOUTH
GAIETY
CONTINUOUS GIRLIE SHOW
MIKE SACHS-STEVE MILLS
VILMA JOZSY D. DARLING
BETTY ROWLAND
VICTOR & BLUEBIRD RECORDS
Benedict's

BETTY: [Rozell] didn't wear a costume, she just wore gold paint at the time, and she did acrobatic dancing in the gold paint.

LIZ: Who would paint her?

BETTY: She painted herself. [CHUCKLES]

LIZ: Every night before the show?

BETTY: Every night—at that time we were doing two shows a day . . . she was always in the gold paint . . . when she went to Europe with the show, that's what intrigued the baron because [he wanted to know] what was under this gold paint. He gave a lot of parties for her, which she didn't go to because she was taking off the paint and didn't feel like going out to a cocktail party.

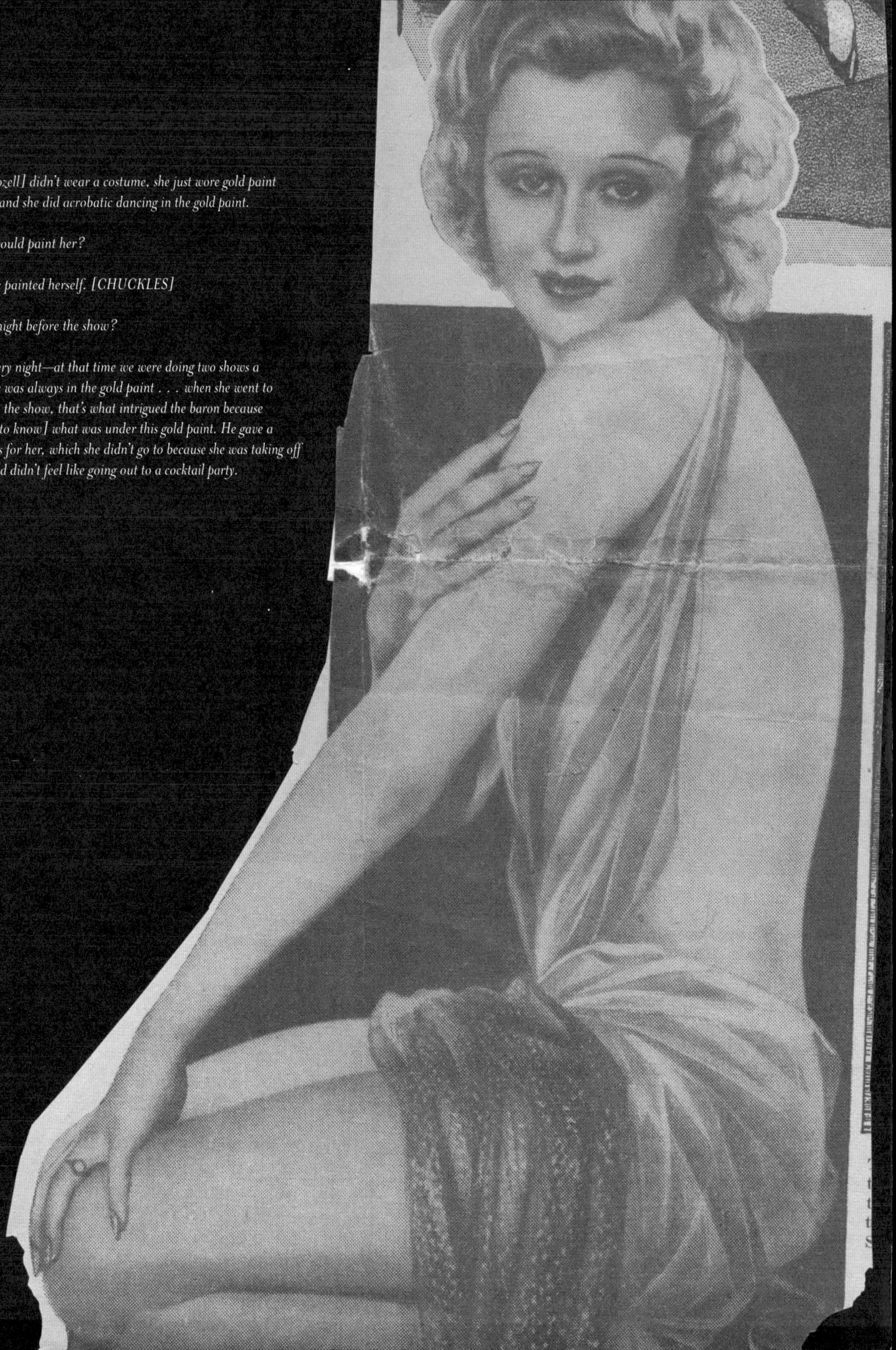

(Foto by Murray Korman

SHE POSES. Long before she married Baron with $10,000,0 annual income, Rose-Zell posed in gilt paint at Irvi ...e Burlesque House.

—Story on pag

SHE HUNTS. After Baron met Rose-Zell in London night club, he took her on long hunting trip into Congo where she trekked it with native beaters in search of big game.

Rozell Rowland wasn't the only burlesque queen who liked to shoot guns—Rose la Rose was also known for her hunting skills.

Rosezell Rowland, former burlesque dancer, was married in Budapest last Thursday to Baron Jean Empain, of Belgium, her mother revealed today.

Gilded Lily of 14th St. Burlesque Weds Baron

Three thousand miles from her $3-a-day burlesque grind on 14th st., glamorous Rozelle Rolland has just married Europe's most glittering multi-millionaire, it was reported today.

Through London came word that the 22-year-old girl, Brooklyn born and bred, has been secretly married in Budapest to Baron Jean Empain, one of the world's richest men, chief owner of the Paris subway, a director in 80 companies and chairman of 30. His income is conservatively computed at more than $10,000,000 a year.

GILDED LILY DAZZLES

Rozelle danced her way up the Arabian Nights path from sordid 14th st. clad in gold paint—and practically nothing else.

At the Irving Place Burlesque she wowed the bald heads when she daubed herself and appeared in a dance number as the "Golden Girl."

She progressed through Broadway to London, where the Baron was captivated at his first glimpse of the dazzling performance.

It was the Baron who, a year ago, was in the public eye as the

"Golden Girl" of Burlesque Weds Wealthy Belgian Baron

Rosezell Rowland, of Brooklyn, Married And Mother Worries About Citizenship

Rosezell Rowland, the Brooklyn girl who won renown a the "Golden Girl" of burlesque in New York, was married i Budapest last Thursday to Baron Jean Empain, multi-mil lionaire Belgian, the girl's mother revealed today.

Only a little over five years ago, when she was 17, Mis Rowland had a $3-a-day job at the Irving Pl. burlesqu theater, appearing clad in gold paint.

This same costume attracted the attention of the youn baron when she appeared in London's Dorchester House, an in February, 1935, a report came from England that the were to be married.

Miss Rowland's mother, Mrs. Alvah B. Rowland, today exhibited a radiogram from the former burlesque star, confirming the marriage.

"Just got married this morning," said the message. "Thanks for consent."

"Baronne Rosezell Empain."

The radiogram was signed "Ba-

PIN-UP GIRLS DAY! IN PERSON BETTY ROWLA
SCREEN • THE MAN WHO WALKED ALONE
Tonight! GUEST STAR NIGHT • EXTRA ACTS • STARS IN PERSON

Amusements
The World of Music

FORMER DANCER Betty Rowland turns comedienne in "Anybody's Girl," at the Beaux Arts.

BURLESQUE STAR Betty Rowland plays her first dramatic role in "Anybody's Girl," opening Thursday at Beaux Arts.

The Theatres

LYRIC

"Night Hawks" is said to be a bright burlesque and vaudeville production that has met with favor in cities wherever it has played. It's a combination of fun, swing, saucy songs and exotic dancing. All these doings will be on tap at the Lyric theatre Monday and Tuesday, with the usual matinees.

Dian Rowland, fascinating dancer, and Bert Carr, quaint Hebrew comedian, share top honors in the show. Others who contribute entertaining features are Billy Ainsley, eccentric tramp in some rollicking fooling that causes laughs galore; Ceil VonDell, Winnie Garrett and Georgia Clyne, strip-teasing lovelies; George Kaye, rich-voiced singer of popular ditties; Charles Harris, talented character actor; Guido and Eva, international ballroom dancers, and a flock of pretty young "Night Hawks" in musical items and tantalizing posings.

"Stepping Sisters"

Mr. and Mrs. Rowland created scrapbooks for all three of their burlesque queen daughters, collecting mementos from their careers while the girls were busy touring across the country.

etty Rowland
gns for Play

etty Rowland, stage dancer, ambitions along the "legiti- te" theater line. She has ed to do a play, "Anybody's ," opening at the Beaux Arts eater Thursday, Feb. 22. Miss vland found the script by nny Day exciting and filled h comedy. However, her big ne, a strip tease, will provide lefinite nostalgic note.

ABOVE:
Betty performs onstage behind Gus Schilling, her unofficial "husband."

OPPOSITE PAGE:
Betty poses with comedian Wally Vernon, a veteran minstrel, vaudeville, and burlesque performer who went on to a "legitimate" career on stage and in film.

LEFT:
Betty poses with actor Forrest Tucker outside her dressing room door. They dated when she first moved to Los Angeles. Another star boyfriend was Orson Welles, who used to stage burlesque shows for his wrap parties.

OPPOSITE PAGE:
There was an art to removing gloves gracefully. According to Gussie Gross, most of the girls preferred "gauntlets," or fingerless gloves, because they were less of a hassle to take off. When wearing gloves with fingers, Betty suggests rolling them down from the top slowly, over your elbow, and then pulling the entire glove off at once, rather than finger by finger. Once the gloves are off, it is imperative to tease with them—swing them around or pull them seductively across your body.

"Society's
Sweetheart"

Dian
Rowland

As luck would have it, Ida and Alva Rowland brought three beautiful burlesque queens into the world: Betty, Rozell, and Dian. A few years older than Betty and Rozell, Dian, born Thelma, was considered the most striking of the sisters, with her platinum hair and large, beguiling eyes.

Betty, who readily agrees that Thelma was always "the prettiest and the best looking" among them, told me the following story from their youth:

Dian headlines at the Gayety Theater in 1943.

BETTY ROWLAND: I saw an ad [in the newspaper for a contest]. I answered, and got my mother to sign [Thelma's] name and enter her in the contest. They sent a letter back that she should be at the Grand Theater or the Southern Theater in Columbus, Ohio, at a [certain] time and they would take her picture . . . at the end of the month the finalist would get dancing lessons and all of these prizes. I wanted to go too. So we went down there . . . it was Thelma's turn and she went in; they did a picture. She came out. Then the lady said [to me], "C'mon, c'mon." And I said, "That's my sister, the one that you just did. We're leaving." And she said, "Get in there." I said, "What am I supposed to do?" So she said, "Just look at the camera and give a wink." And so I looked at the camera and gave a wink. So the end of the week came along and I won . . . Thelma didn't.

LIZ: Was your sister mad?

BETTY ROWLAND: Oh, no. She didn't want to do it anyway. But it was a "naughty wink" contest. I didn't know what we were doing in there. So I was kind of half mad at that lady for pushing me in there. And I guess I gave a wicked wink and it came out very good. [LAUGHS]

Unfortunately, Thelma was born with a heart condition that prevented her from joining Betty in the dancing lessons she won as the prize for the "naughty wink" contest. So when the girls went "professional," Rozell and Betty became a dancing sister act and left Thelma to strike out on her own. As Betty recalls, "Thelma didn't look good on the marquee," so the first step in Thelma's transformation into a star was a name change in homage to the Greek goddess of the moon, Diana, a legendary ethereal beauty. For distinction, she dropped the "e" from Diane and christened herself "Dian Rowland."

Dian was tall and lovely and quickly got work as a showgirl, or parade girl, in stage shows. Not long after cutting her teeth as a parade girl, her sinuous body and platinum blonde hair attracted the notice of producers looking for new burlesque acts. She was on her way to top billing.

Dian's act was characterized by her refined, graceful movements. With her fragile heart she couldn't do acrobatic dancing like Rozell, or ballet like Betty. Instead, she sashayed around the stage in shimmering gowns, her beauty on full display. Betty considered Dian's act comparable to those of Las Vegas showgirls: "They just parade around with a pretty costume . . . [Later Dian] got into stripping too. Not dance stripping. All she had to be was herself she was so gorgeous."

Dian's best-known number was called "The Dance of Perfection." Her devotees were truly moved by her serene performances, as is evident in the following fan letter: "You should rank among the greatest dancers of all time—namely, Anna Pavlova, Marguerite Agniel, Ruth St. Denis, Isadora Duncan and yourself."

Dian's glamorous stage presence led her to fame as "society's sweetheart." She booked society shows, private club dinners, and nightclub appearances in addition to theater dates across the United States and Canada where she would do up to four shows a day, six days a week. Dian headlined the Old Howard, The Gaiety, The National, and countless other venues, gaining masses of fans wherever she appeared. Her iconic face was plastered across newspapers advertising the latest burlesque shows, and sensational write-ups were published whenever she came into town to perform.

Her stacks of fan mail attest to her drawing power. Among her fan mail is a letter dated January 1943 from the Harvard Club asking if she would be their dinner guest. The author of the letter, a Harvard Club fraternity brother, wrote: "My pledge class has voted you the most exotic burlesque star of the year."

During World War II at the height of her fame, Dian was a morale booster for homesick troops. At one War Bond Rally in June 23, 1944, she was billed as "The Lovely exotic dancer," sandwiched in between "Buster Shaver with Olive, George and Richard—midgets from the tiny town revue" and "Charles Carlisle and Frankie Rapp—Famous Duo of Wits."

A letter from a World War II sergeant, who saw her performance in Montreal, reads: "I am being posted back to England. I understand, on night fighters, it is the custom of ops. pilots to carry with them a good luck charm and although you will think I have an awful nerve I am going to take the chance of being rebuffed . . . will you please send me as a good luck charm one of those delightfully small and flimsy articles with which you attempted to hide your charms before the actual finale of your second turn." (Had he known the cost of Dian's wardrobe, he might not have been so bold!)

Some men waxed poetic in their letters to Dian: "I am at present rehearsing a radio script in Newark. I had a few hours to kill before rehearsal time, so, as there was a slight mist in Newark on Wednesday, I ducked into the Empire and caught the show. I mean to say I saw you. For that I am eternally grateful to the mist. Before you appeared I was bored by a succession of girls whose sense of the exotic consisted of a series of bumps and grinds. I may be wrong, perhaps I was overcome by the cigar smoke, but it is my humble opinion that you are the most wondrous thing that has been put together in quite some time."

For all her love letters and well-wishers, Dian died alone on the road while she was working at a theater in Detroit. When she didn't show up for her spot one night, someone went to check on her and found her dead in her hotel room. The coroner report stated the cause of death to be a heart attack. Her sister Betty recalls, "I just got a call one day [from a fellow stripper, who said] 'Your sister didn't come to work.' Everybody was concerned about her 'cause she was always on time. In that business you have to have discipline and be there. . . . And then I was getting ready to go to work and [I got the call that she was dead]. Her heart just [gave out]. It was quite a shock. She was in Detroit and it was pretty warm there, I guess, and maybe it was just too much for her. She was only twenty-nine."

Very little information about Dian Rowland survives today. Her brief life is captured in the scrapbooks lovingly created by her parents and her sister Betty's recollections. Sadly, Dian's short life was hardly an anomaly among burlesque queens. Tough working conditions, life on the road, and a career contingent on the beauty of youth made the fame of a burlesque queen as ephemeral as the image of lovely Dian.

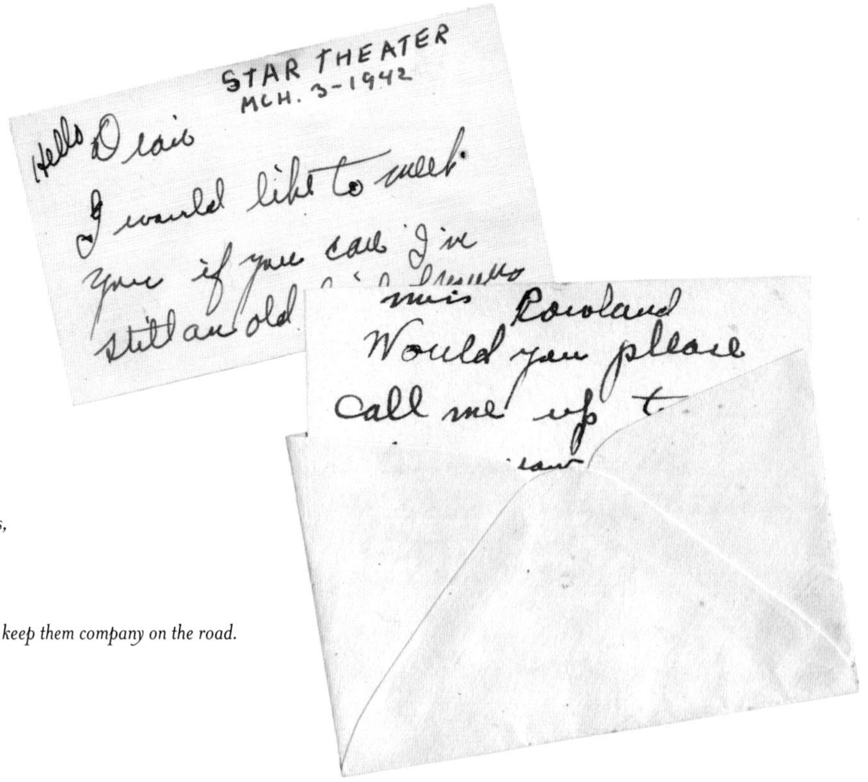

Notes from an admirer sent backstage along with flowers, asking if Dian might care to go to supper with him.

OPPOSITE PAGE:
Many girls on the burlesque circuit traveled with dogs to keep them company on the road.

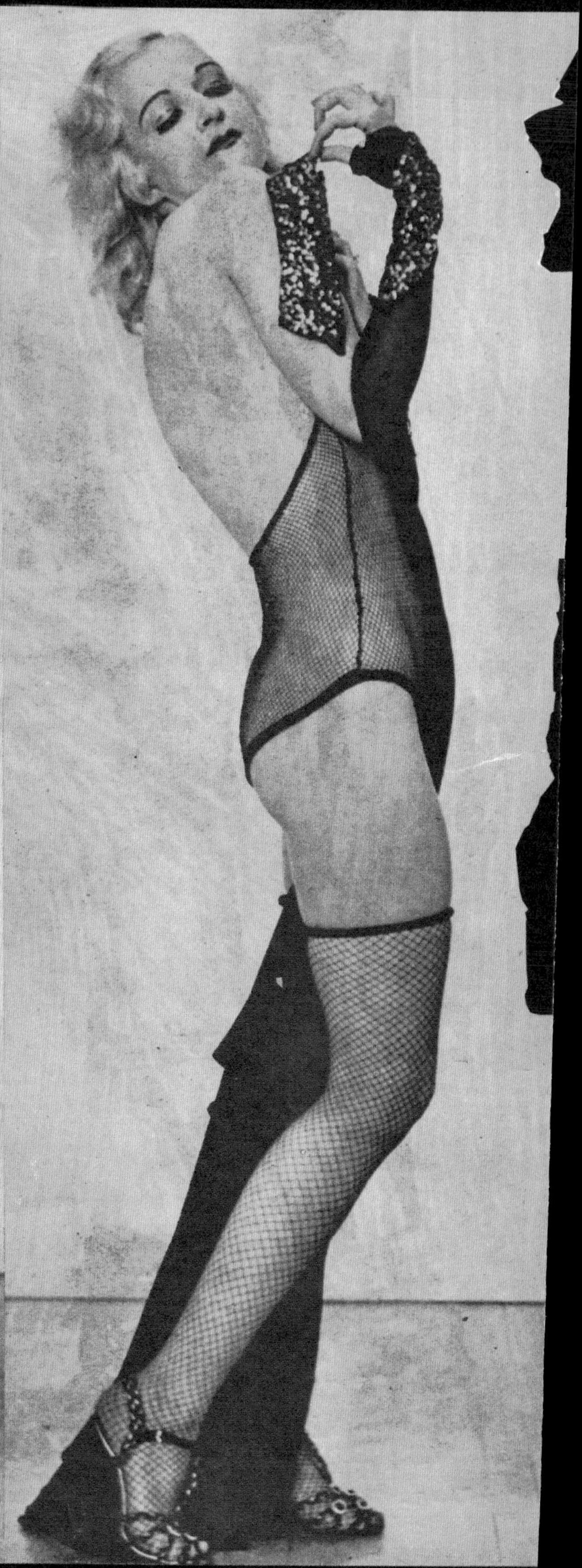

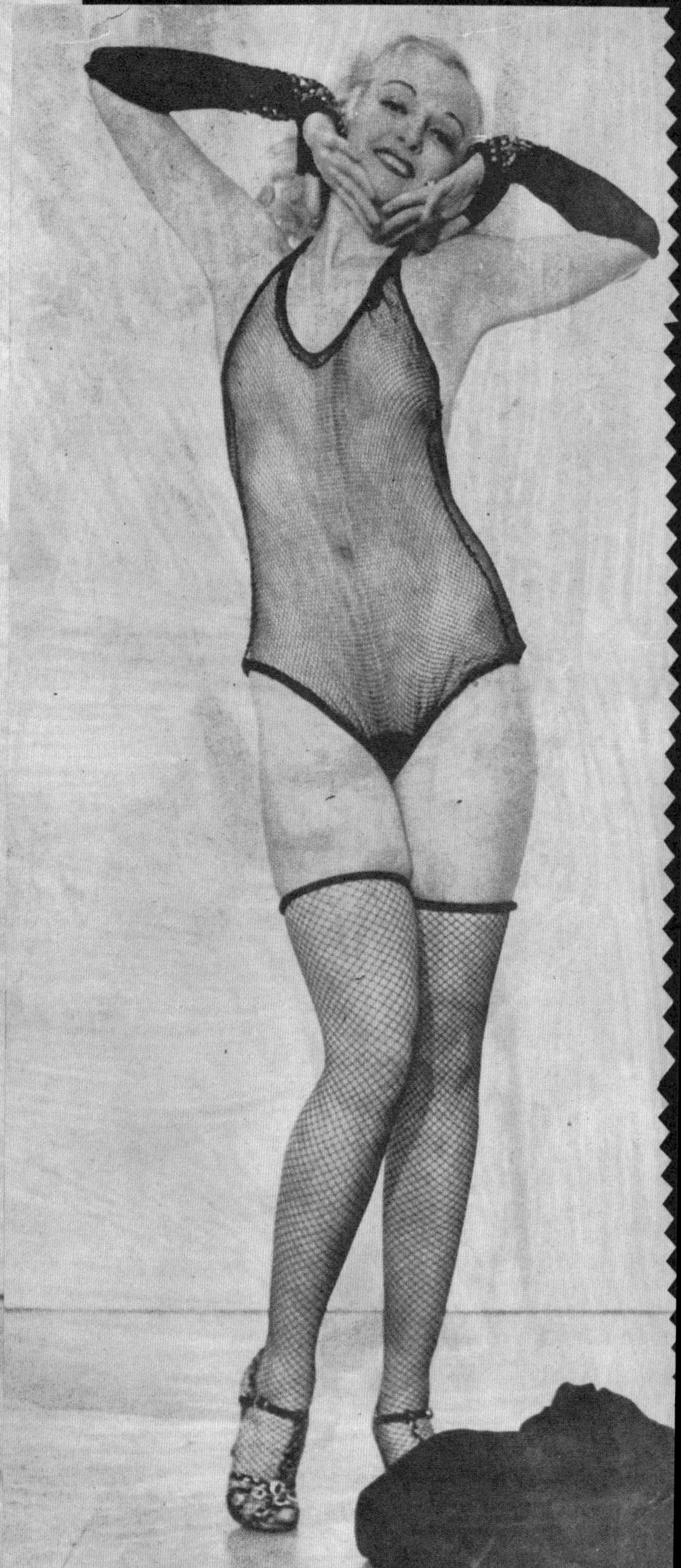

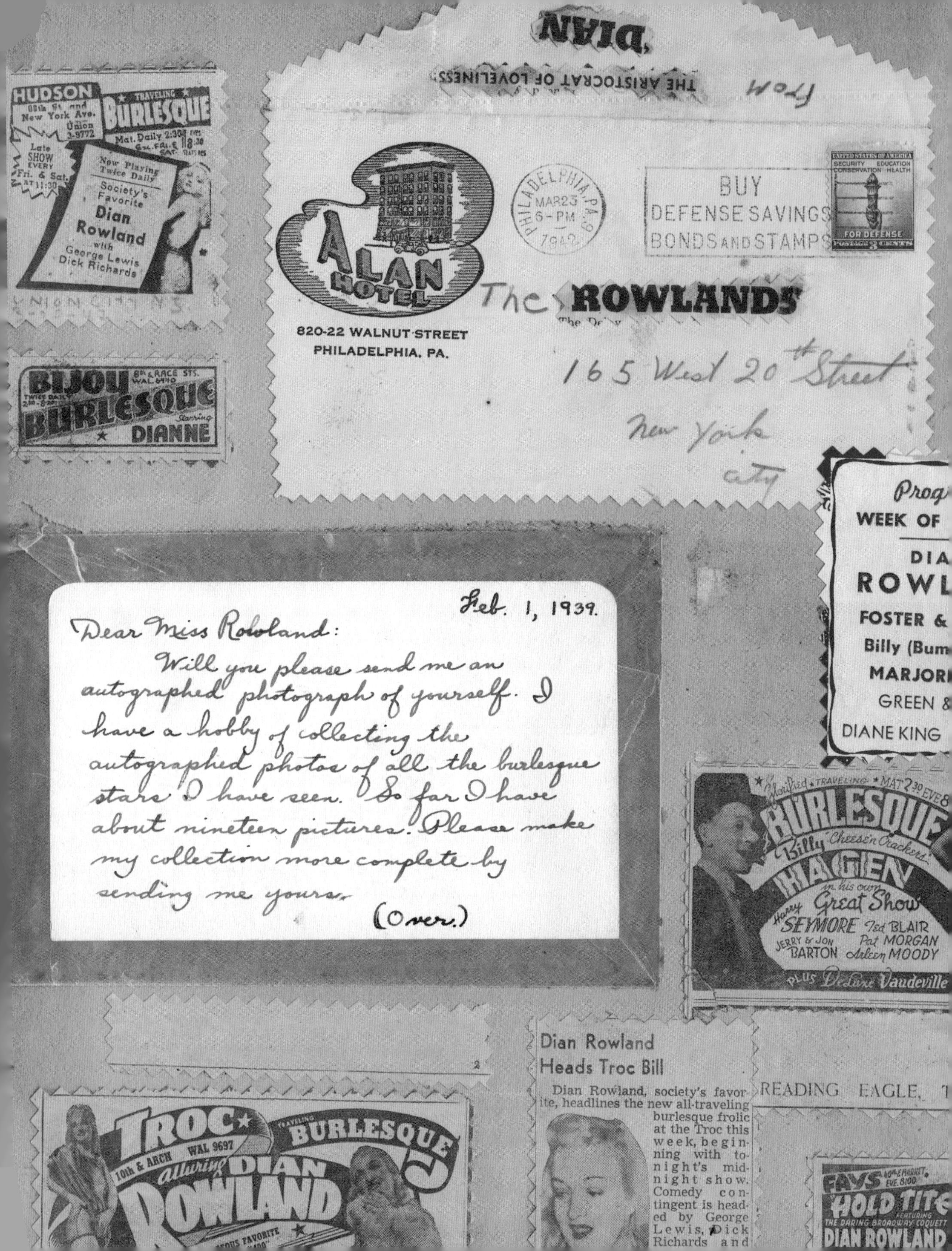

Feb. 1, 1939.

Dear Miss Rowland:

Will you please send me an autographed photograph of yourself. I have a hobby of collecting the autographed photos of all the burlesque stars I have seen. So far I have about nineteen pictures. Please make my collection more complete by sending me yours.

(Over.)

2

Dian Rowland
Heads Troc Bill

Dian Rowland, society's favorite, headlines the new all-traveling burlesque frolic at the Troc this week, beginning with tonight's midnight show. Comedy contingent is headed by George Lewis, Dick Richards and

READING EAGLE, T

DAY MORNING. MARCH 22, 1942

Dian Rowland at Troc

The burlesque at the Troc stars Dian Rowland. The comedy is headed

HO

RPHEUM
READING
WED.,
PRIL 8
4-1769
TS RESERVED
ty's Sweetheart
ITIFUL
IAN
wland
nal NET GIRL
TS NOW
N SALE

DING TIMES, READING, PA.,

APR AY MORNING, APRIL 7, 1942

Glorified ★ TRAVELING ★ MAT 2:30 EVE 8:30
BURLESQUE
"Billy" "Cheese'n Crackers"
HAGEN
in his own

ORPHEUM
READING
WED.,
APRIL 8
Dial 4-1769
ALL SEATS RESERVED
Society's Sweetheart

darling Dean Rowland

Taken at:
Troc Theatre, Philadelphia, Pa
September 10, 1940

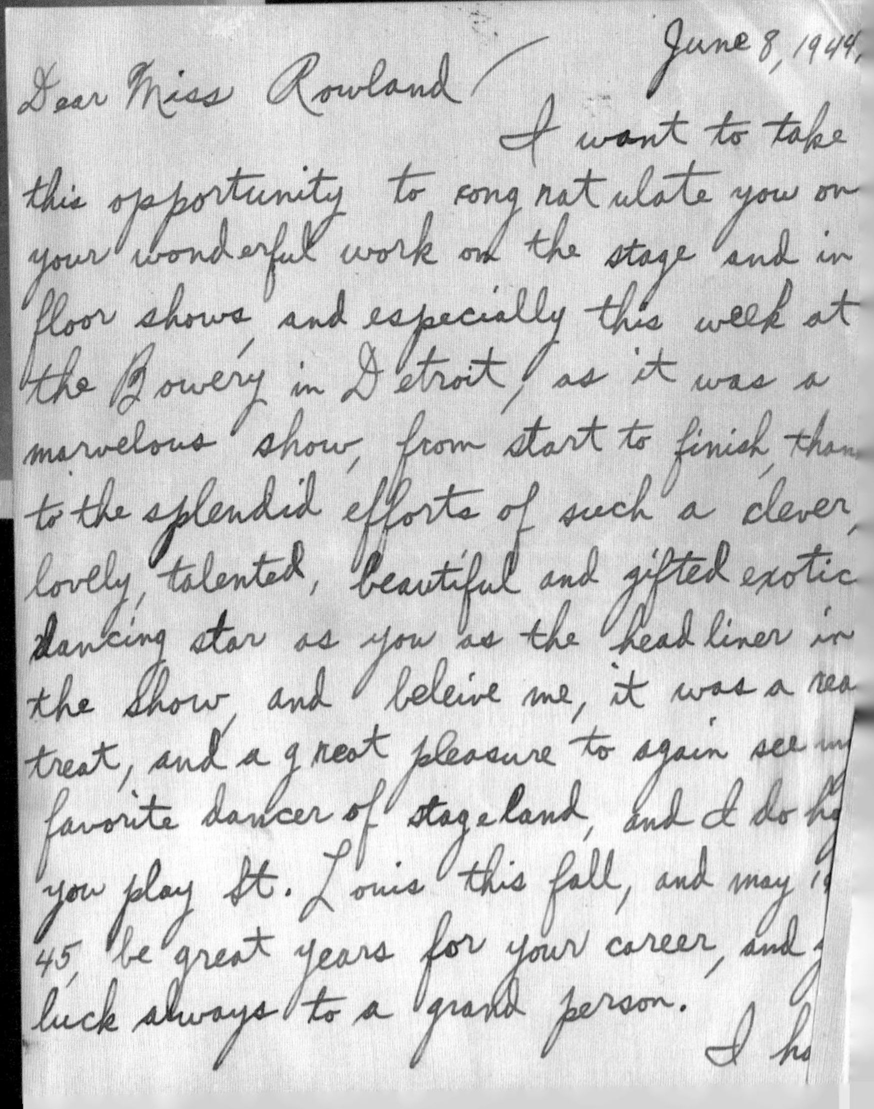

June 8, 1944,

Dear Miss Rowland,

I want to take this opportunity to cong rat ulate you on your wonderful work on the stage and in floor shows and especially this week at the Bowery in Detroit, as it was a marvelous show, from start to finish, than to the splendid efforts of such a clever, lovely, talented, beautiful and gifted exotic dancing star as you as the headliner in the Show, and beleive me, it was a rea treat, and a great pleasure to again see m favorite dancer of stageland, and I do ho you play St. Louis this fall, and may 1 45, be great years for your career, and luck always to a grand person.

I ho

An awed gentleman wrote the following to Dian after seeing her show: "So about 4:50 I went to the Gaiety Theatre. Well I saw the star. A picture of stunning enchantment. She looked like some society girls, only much more beautiful."

June St. Clair

"The Platinum Princess"

In Rex Huntington's archive, I found a photo of a beautiful blonde burlesque queen with the handwritten note, "June St. Clair." The beguiling image made me wonder about her fate. While searching through my notes to see if anyone had spoken of June, I remembered a story Sherry Britton had told me during an interview in response to my question, "Was the myth that strippers were promiscuous false?" To illustrate that not all burlesque strippers were promiscuous, she told me about a woman she knew on the road called June St. Clair: "[I] became close to two sisters. One of them was a beautiful, lovely, gentle blonde girl who traveled with her mother. Her name was June St. Clair. When her mother died, she was thirty-five years old and she was a virgin. She had never had a date. Of course, that led to a tragedy because she fell in love with this young man who didn't treat her very well. And she committed suicide."

Jerry (June) and her brother Frank, to whom she wrote her suicide note.

Haunted by Sherry's story and the only picture I had seen of June, I was troubled not to be able to find more information on June's life and her tragic fate. In a strange stroke of luck, after my 2005 documentary film *Pretty Things* premiered in the United States, a woman named Lane Willingham contacted me, wanting to know if I had any information about her aunt, a former burlesque queen whose stage name was June St. Clair. Lane said that June's career had been a "well-kept family secret," and that her father, June's brother Frank, "had never seen her act, probably out of embarrassment." Lane turned over a treasure trove of June's letters and personal photographs, hoping to piece together more information about her family. From these letters and recollections of other queens who knew her, the elusive story of this beautiful blonde woman began to emerge.

June St. Clair was born Geraldine Margaret Ford on October 6, 1913, and lived most of her childhood in a small town in Massachusetts.

June, her mother, her sister Helen, and an unidentified friend.

Along with her younger sister Helen and her older brother Frank, Geraldine (who went by "Jerry") lived in a two-story Victorian house with chickens in the garden. Their parents, both of whom were Irish Catholic, spoke with a thick Irish brogue. Their father worked in shoe factories in Boston, but lost his job when the Depression hit. June had just graduated from the tenth grade and Helen from the eighth grade when their father moved to New York City to find work. Soon after, the girls quit school and went to New York with their mother to look for work as well. Frank stayed in Massachusetts to finish his schooling and later joined the military.

In New York, June started out as a coat-check girl to make ends meet. To increase their earning potential, she and her sister decided to try their luck at show business and landed work as chorus girls in burlesque. June, who had always been considered beautiful, was picked out of the line and featured on a swing in the finale number. Perched high above the other showgirls and the audience, June posed on her swing, a picture of female beauty, while Helen stayed in the background in the chorus. June soon earned a regular solo spot and rose up the ranks to burlesque queen status.

Their mother traveled with them, and they tried to work jobs on the same show so that they could all be together. Sherry Britton, who performed on the same burlesque circuit, told me, "Their mother was a little old Irish lady who traveled with them. Never heard her say a word. Not a word. She was a little gray-haired [lady] with a knot on top. Round cherubic face. [One time they were playing] in Holyoke, their hometown. They had told the family the reason they were traveling so much was they worked for a cosmetics company and they were selling cosmetics. Suddenly, a note came backstage from a family member, in Holyoke. And when the mother saw it, she said, 'Jesus, Joseph and Mary, we're in the shit house now!' The only words I ever heard her speak—before or after!"

It was in burlesque that Jerry took her stage name, "June St. Clair," and Helen became "Helen Colby." Whereas many burlesque queens adopted their stage names for their personal lives as well, there was a clear distinction between June St. Clair and Jerry. June was a character who danced onstage for money. Jerry was a loyal daughter and sister (she sent her brother Frank ten dollars a week toward his college tuition) who hated having to compromise her modesty and reveal her body to earn a living. She wished she could work in Hollywood films or in dramatic roles. She had been offered a place in summer stock on the East Coast but didn't take it because the pay was low—twenty dollars per week plus room and board. Later, when she was stuck on the road, she regretted not taking the position. She wrote to her brother about the future of the sister act: "Where we'll wind up—nobody knows. But nothing ventured—nothing gained."

By 1937, June was starring solo in burlesque shows as the featured stripper and her appearances were advertised with her moniker, "The Platinum Princess." She traveled across the big wheel in the United States, playing all over the East and West Coasts, crossing paths with the biggest comedians such as Manny King and Bozo Snyder, as well as fellow burlesque queens. Betty Rowland, who knew June, remembers her as a "sweet, quiet girl with a good sense of humor. June didn't like to strip at all. She had small breasts and waist with 'Grecian' hips and derriere. When she took off her skirt the men would go crazy. She would exit and not come back out [onstage] for more applause—ever."

June had difficulty reconciling her career as a stripteaser. From her letters, it is evident that her priorities lay with her family. She wrote often to her younger brother Frank, begging him to visit her on the road. Her letters were usually on hotel stationery, as the "girls" moved around frequently—every few weeks a new city, another hotel and theater. In one letter to Frank, June complained about the show she was in: "They have taken all the nice people from this show and replaced them with drunkards and riff-raff. The straight man [comic] we have now has body odor and liquor breath constantly. Helen and I do a scene with him—and in it—Helen must sit on his lap—she looks as

June and Helen in their sister act "The Ford Sisters," which wasn't as successful as June's solo career.

though she is holding her breath and going to faint from the effort. And if that isn't enough B.O. for one show—we have the 'Beef Trust,' too. Six fat girls all over 250 pounds each—and when they thunder past to make an entrance the stench is really devastating."

In another letter to Frank, she wrote about her drinking, which occasionally got out of control. After describing a recent bender, she declared, "I am back on my budget of a cocktail before dinner and on special occasions two or three—and that's for life. I wasn't cut out to be a drinkin' woman." June added that she went on "a crying jag . . . because a newspaper fellow I knew committed suicide."

There were occasional good times; Sherry says a highlight of her own burlesque career was a vacation she took with Helen and June in Atlantic City. Both Sherry and Betty recall June's good sense of humor despite her inner turmoil.

Perhaps because Helen had difficulty making it as a solo artist, or June missed her sister's company on the road, the girls formed a sister act. They called themselves the Ford Sisters, which was also the name of an earlier, famous vaudeville duo. They did pretty well as a team—if booked into a nightclub, they could earn about $600 for twelve days of work, minus a 15 percent commission to their booking agent and the railroad fares to the gig. The hours, though, were hard: 8:30 P.M. to 4:30 A.M. three shows a night, seven days a week. The sisters performed across the United States and even in Montreal where, in a letter to their brother Frank, Helen wrote that because the native language is French, the comedians "never get a laugh on their jokes, only on their falls or any comedic movements." They worked theaters alongside such stars as Gypsy Rose Lee, who apparently had a beef with June. It is rumored that, in a statement to the Associated Press, June said Gypsy was a fraud and that her work shouldn't be considered "art."

In 1946 June and Helen's mother died, leaving them to traverse the country without her. June wrote in a letter to Frank, "I think of Mama constantly. Time doesn't seem to lessen my sense of loss, but rather to intensify it. Perhaps, it's because she has been with me in all these theaters, hotels and restaurants—so many times." In the same letter, she tells her brother she has been reading *The Razor's Edge* by Somerset Maugham. She was interested in the idea of transmigration (reincarnation), which the book explores: "It's very impressive and seems to me quite a credible theory—even though it doesn't give one as much to look forward to as Catholicism does—perhaps that's why more intellectuals believe in transmigration. It's really something to imagine though—that I might have been a poor hunchback in some other life and might be a sea captain in one that is yet to come . . . "

By 1948, June was performing solo again, and was booked to play the Follies Theater in Los Angeles. She complained of being homesick and said in a letter to Frank that Los Angeles was beautiful if "one has a car and lots of money. . . . But this downtown section of Los Angeles is the same as any other city and Main Street—where the theater is situated—is a terrible street." June wrote that she was still a "pale face" because "the sun doesn't shine into these dressing rooms." Still, she was grateful to have a job, admitting that it was getting harder and harder to find work in burlesque: "Business—show business—has taken a decided slump—all over the country."

Both Betty and Sherry said that June never dated men. In one of June's letters to Frank, she talks about going to the movies with a man who got upset when she wouldn't hold his hand in the theater. Betty thinks that June's innocence about sex is what led to her suicide. She said June met a man in Chicago and started dating him—only to get pregnant and find out the man was married. According to Betty, June was ashamed and humiliated (Betty notes that June did not realize that this was happening every day all over the world to women) and became so distraught that she killed herself.

June's niece Lane also believes that June's story involved a married man, and that this man might have raped her. In a suicide note left to her brother Frank, June speaks of being "ashamed." Lane says that her father, Frank, told her that Jerry once came to visit the family with a man she was dating, "presumably the one who was abusing her . . . It seems that after my grandmother [June's mother] died, Jerry met and fell in love with this man, who was the son of a theater owner, and he turned out to be married. He was abusing Jerry and raped her and the shame of all of that was just too much for her, having been a devoted Catholic and a virgin all those years."

Apparently, June had tried to commit suicide three times. The first time, she slit her wrists at a hotel in New York City. The second time, she was discovered with rocks in her pocket in a garden near a quarry where she intended to drown herself. Finally, she was found dead on October 21, 1949, in a hotel room in Manhattan. There is some uncertainty about how June finally killed herself; Lane remem-

An ad for June's star act at the Rialto.

bers hearing it was an overdose of pills, while Sherry thinks that June choked to death after purposely swallowing some kind of object that obstructed her breathing. June's death certificate dated October 26, 1949, states the cause of death to be "congestion of the viscera: pending chemical examination." Even on her death certificate, the circumstances of June's life are cloudy—this document refers to her age at death as both "34 years old" and "36." In fact, June was thirty-five.

Lane says, "I never liked asking my father about it because he was the one who was called to identify her body and I'm sure it was a horrible time for him." According to Lane, Helen blamed herself for her sister's suicide and was never the same. Sherry, who was friends with both women, said, "Helen became a recluse. She lived on Fifty-fifth Street . . . and after her sister's death, she became a little strange, and said that she was the wife of Jesus." Lane says Helen was diagnosed with dementia and was later placed in a home in New Jersey.

It is a tragic ending to what appears on the surface of June and Helen's glossy 8 x 10s to have been rather glamorous lives; too often burlesque queens and showgirls ended up this way. I once spoke to Nils Hanson, historian and president of The Ziegfeld Club, about how the same stage door Johnnies who promised to take them away from life on the stage often betrayed Ziegfeld Girls. Nils read me a portion of a letter he received from a Ziegfeld Girl in 1966, pleading for assistance because she was broke: "I'm sorry I have to say I've been harassed, impoverished and betrayed. This all by someone who should have proved himself fine and honest. As well, my daughter's soul and health of mind and body have suffered so at 22 because of him. She's a shadow of her wonderful lovingness and tender radiance. She is practically a walking dead person as I see it. She is powerless and at his mercy. My nightmares continue on and on."

Nils said it made him "sad to see . . . that they've fallen on such hard times, when they were really worshipped by the theater-going public during the height of their beauty. It's really a sad commentary on what happens to these women after having lived such glamorous lives and knowing everybody who was important, and at the end are forgotten."

Nils' patient documentation of the Ziegfeld Girls' stories keeps their memories alive. Similarly, June's voice has been preserved here and in the letters she left behind. And above all, her memory will always remain linked to the faded photographs of an everlasting beauty.

Take care of my Helen

My Vroni—

Forgive me —

I have throughout my life — loved you so. My happiest thought now is that you & Helen will profit by my mistakes —— and live your lives as happily as you can There is no hope for me — because I feel my mind is shot to bits. I cannot come back to the happiness I knew once. I have disgraced you all — please find it in your heart to forgive me. I love you & Micah & Lane — so much even tho I cannot proove it now. J.

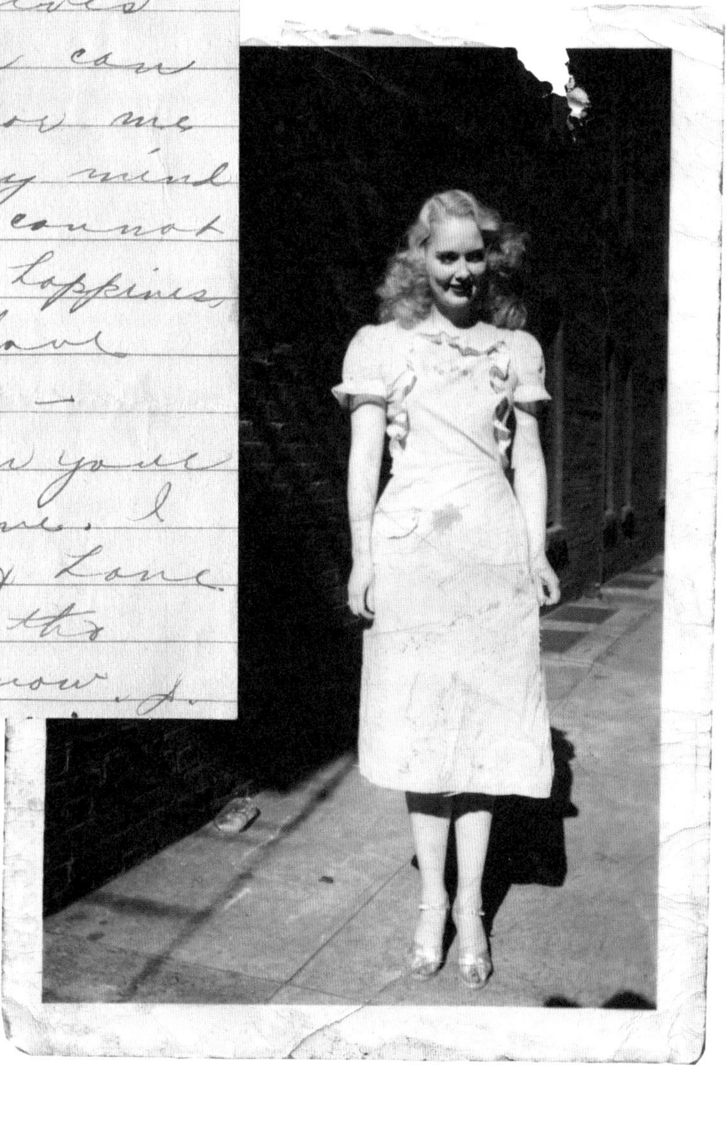

I tank aye go home

In the garbage can

Dolores, Tommy Raft & I
in the stage door way

this was taken against
my better judgment

To Paul Morokoff
All my best
wishes. Just wishing
you what I wish myself
the best of everything.
Yours Truly
Tommy Bozo Snyder
Toronto Canada
Nov 24/193

June St. Clair and Tommy "Bozo" Snyder often worked the same shows. Tommy Snyder was a comedian who started out in vaudeville and was known as one of the great pantomimists of burlesque theater. He wrote, directed, produced, and starred in the play Bozo *which was performed at the Gaiety Theater in Boston in 1927. The name stuck as he signed his photograph "Tommy Bozo Snyder" to burlesque choreographer and producer Paul Morokoff ten years later.*

OPPOSITE PAGE (TOP):
June and a gentleman at a nightclub. June noted on the photo her new cigarette case and her glass of limeade, but not the name of her companion.

OPPOSITE PAGE (BOTTOM): *June seems weary from the hard life on the road.*

limeade

LEFT: *A smoldering portrait of the Platinum Princess.* BELOW: *A young and innocent June.*

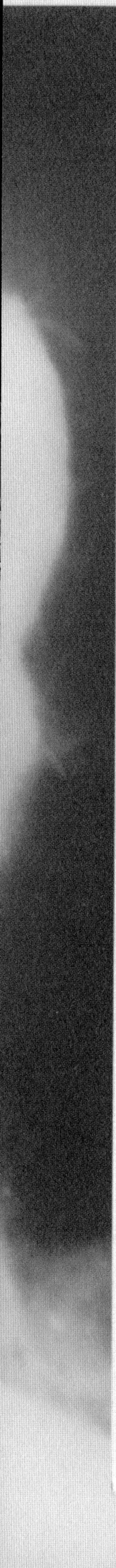

Lois de Fee
"The Amazon of Burlesque"

"To Abie"
With Best always to
a swell person
Lois de Fee
Cavell / NY

In the late 1930s, Lois de Fee worked as a bouncer at nightclubs in New York City, where her presence and size made her a fearsome security guard. As her friend Zorita describes her, "Lois is loud, boisterous and had a mouth on her . . . " Years later, her forceful nature hasn't softened much. Though she now lives in a retirement home, she punched out a friend of hers for "yapping" during the premiere of my documentary film, *Pretty Things*.

As Lois puts it, "I was born with a stage name, so why not [use it]?" Born in a small town in Texas, Lois's mother died when she was two years old and her father passed away when she was seven. Her aunt took her in after her mother died, which was not an ideal family situation. Lois says, "My uncle cheated on my aunt all the time and she made me very aware of sex. She used to lift me up to look over the transom [in hotel rooms where he would meet his lovers] to see if he was in bed with one of his girlfriends." Lois says that her aunt "had a temper and she took it out on me. I didn't like getting spanked. When she'd have a fight with her husband she'd beat up on me. And I resented it."

She tried to run away to "the big city" several times—the first time when she was only four years old. She was given dancing lessons until she was eight or nine, then her aunt stopped them because she thought Lois was putting on airs. Lois says she had told her dance teacher that her name was going to be in lights on Broadway. "I didn't even know where Broadway was. But oddly enough, when I did open in burlesque, the first time, it was at Forty-sixth and Broadway and my name was in lights on Broadway. So my young prophecy came true."

Lois ran away for good at age thirteen. She found a job at a club in Miami on Fourteenth Street, where the owner was looking for showgirls to take to Cuba. Despite her age, Lois says, "Brass monkey me, I walked right in and got the job." Once they got to Cuba, Lois

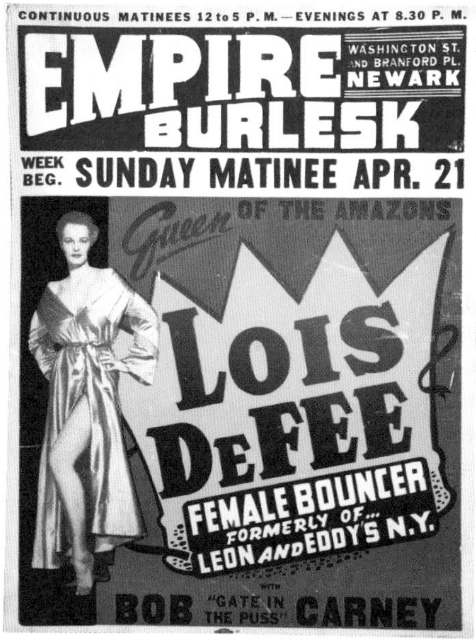

Empire Burlesk poster. After Mayor La Guardia outlawed burlesque in New York City in 1939, other cities followed suit. Theater owners used creative spelling to get around local ordinances, such as "burlesk" and "burley-que."

recalls that the producer "found out I had two left feet and I couldn't dance nothing." He then modified her role to parading in the opening, and in the finale Lois stood perfectly still as a "nude statue on black velvet steps." The show played in Cuba for several months, but when it was supposed to open in Miami at the Olympic Theater, Lois missed the train stop and kept going all the way to New York City. She said she never had any problems traveling by herself at such a young age, possibly due to her imposing height and tough attitude. She says, "When I look back, I'd have been dead, with the things that go on today. But no one ever made the first bad step toward me. Truckers picked me up and dropped off, fed me, and told me to go home. Nothing, nothing bad ever happened to me."

When Lois arrived in New York, she looked up a man she had met in Miami. His brother owned The Dizzy Club nightclub, and Lois was given a job as the bouncer. The publicity stunt of having a female bouncer gave Lois instant fame. She recalls, "[Tabloid reporter] Walter Winchell had a line in his column about me and it just seemed to roll over from there." In 1933, she started working at Leon & Eddie's nightclub, also as a bouncer.

In 1939 Lois got a job at the New York World's Fair as "Queen of the Amazons" in the Amazon exhibit. Burlesque producer Al Minksy approached her there and offered her a job as a featured act at one of his venues. Of course, the new job would require Lois to do a striptease. She had never seen a striptease and hadn't the faintest idea how to do one, but they were offering $400 a week, which was just too good to pass up. She saw seventeen shows in one week, got the gist, and opened at the Gaiety Theater on Broadway on Friday, October 13, 1939.

She and Sherry Britton met for the first time at the Gaiety, though they recall different versions of the event. Sherry said that Harold Minsky, the owner of the Gaiety, brought Lois to her: "She had been a bouncer in the nightclubs on Fifty-second Street. He told me to make a stripper of her. So I did, which is funny, and I taught her to strip. We became quite close friends." In Lois's version, she says, "I was the star right away. I never did any spot but star spot. Sherry was third spot on the first show that I was on there at the Gaiety. I was the star of the show and she was third spot. And that's how I met Sherry."

Lois didn't do a bump and grind routine or "milk" the audience by sticking a leg or arm out through the curtain. She always did her

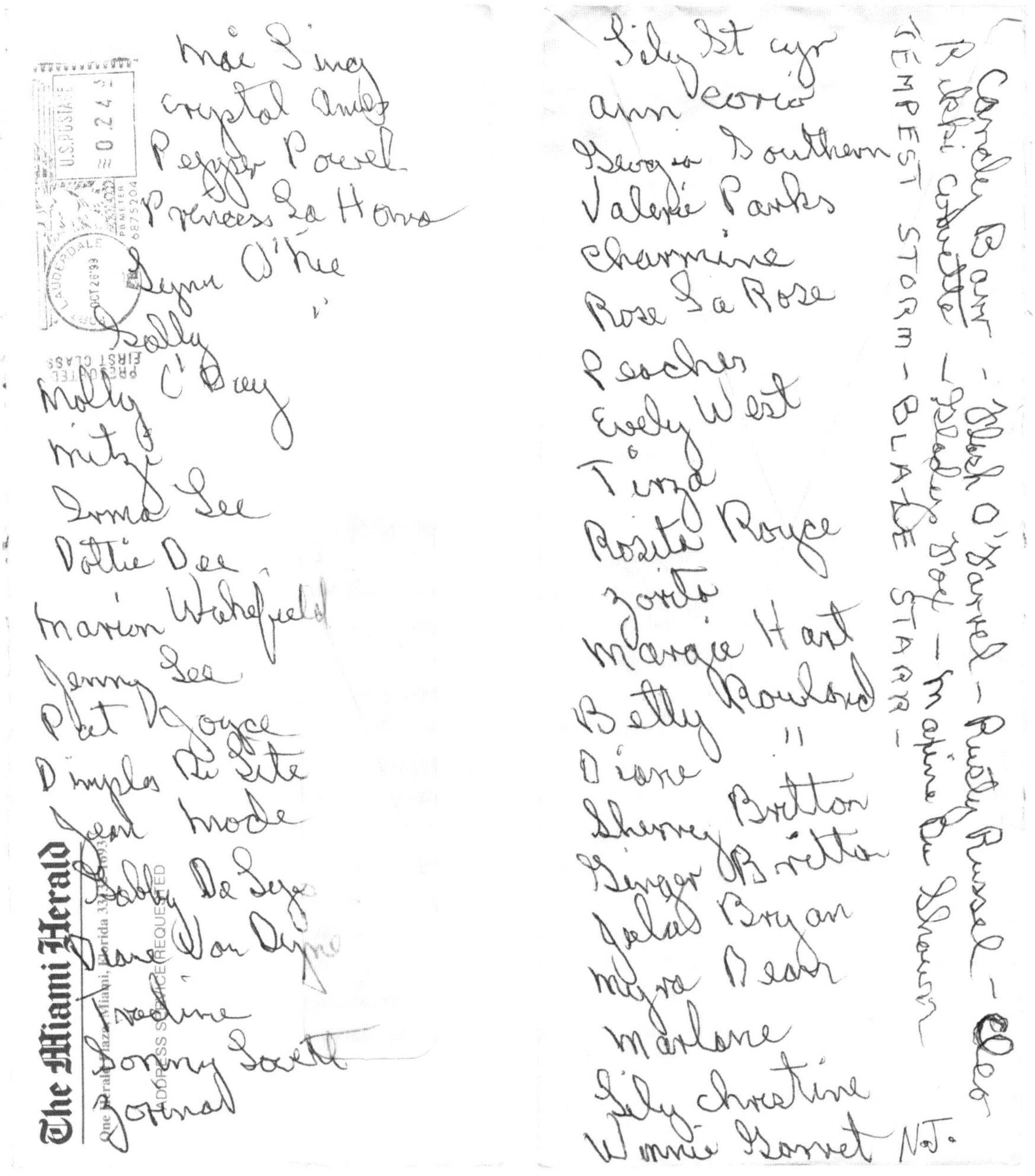

Lois gave me this list of all the burlesque queens she knew.

Lois wears an elegant burlesque costume made of Spanish lace.

own thing and it worked. With her regal air and stature, Lois became known as the "First Lady of Burlesque," grandly parading around in a "Ziegfeld manner"—a showgirl turned stripper. She used jazz standards like "Sophisticated Lady," "Little White Gardenia," and "Solitude" for her music and threw white gardenias out to the audience. She calls her strip "ladylike," and says her costumes were so demure that she would have her maid sew her up in them when she finished her routine and wear them out nightclubbing. Her costumes were Grecian style, made by Billy Livingston, who designed for Brooks Costumes at the time.

Lois had many male admirers, and it was reported that she was married seven times, though she is cagey when pressed for an accurate number. She says, "The papers said seven times, but I wasn't married seven times. But you didn't argue with papers. You went with the flow." Lois's scrapbook holds quite a collection of photos of handsome young men. When I asked about one man in particular, she said, "A guy. You can't remember all their names, honey!" She was married to an army officer during World War II but she said they divorced because "he liked my chorus girls on my show and I didn't like that." In addition to her countless husbands, Lois received hundreds of fan letters a week and gifts from stage door Johnnies. Pointing to a scrapbook photo of herself wearing an elaborate metal headpiece, she told me, "See this headpiece here? The Indian prince gave that to me. Prince Jit of Capathela, India."

Lois and Zorita sometimes disagreed over who received the most attention from high-profile playboys. Lois says that John Jacob Astor used to send her ten $100 bills a month in admiration of her talents. Zorita counters, "Lois is full of shit," and says that Astor was a cheapskate:

> John Jacob Astor came in the club one night with a very charming blonde and he asked me to come over to the table. So I went over to the table and sat with him and drank my usual champagne, which was a lot of nothing. And on the way out he put a twenty-dollar bill in my hand and said, "Call me, I'm in the book." So after he'd left I looked at this [bill]—*Twenty dollars. Really*. Well, I don't need his twenty dollars. I sent it to Walter Winchell. "Dear Walter, The other night John Jacob Astor came in and said his principal reason

for coming was my snake and its health. I assured him that my snake was happy and healthy. Leaving he slipped me a twenty-dollar bill and said 'Call me I'm in the book.' Walter, honey, do you think he really wants to talk about snakes?"

Lois became accustomed to men masturbating in the audience during her performances and takes a more lighthearted view than other queens have on this subject.

> LOIS: I think [the first time I noticed masturbation] was at the Gaiety, and Casey was the drummer. And they didn't have a curtain between the orchestra and the first row. I heard giggling so I became conscious something was going on below. And Casey was saying to this guy, "Am I keeping the right rhythm for you? You want me to go any faster? Or is this too slow?" The guy was masturbating and Casey was ribbing him about it. [LAUGHS] That was the first time.
>
> LIZ: And did you treat it as a joke or did it upset you or—
>
> LOIS: No, it didn't upset me. Because he's out there and I'm there; you don't meet. It's like it's another world. It's like a clear glass is between you and the audience. You can see and you know but it doesn't have any effect.

When Pearl Harbor was bombed in 1941, Lois was onstage at the Star Theater in Brooklyn. She hadn't heard the news yet, but when the audience started walking out, she remembers thinking to herself, "*Oh, my God, am I that bad?* and I was almost crying. I thought it was me that they were walking out on. And when I get offstage the stagehands are laughing. They said, 'No, they just bombed Pearl Harbor; they didn't walk out because of you.'"

During World War II Lois hit her stride and became one of the reigning queens. In 1941 Charlie Barnett and his orchestra dedicated a song to her, called "Lois." Though she received many letters from GIs abroad, Lois said that she "had a tremendous following among women . . . I guess because of the type of strip that I did. In fact, the greatest compliment that I ever had was during the World War II era and I just was working at the Hudson Theater in New Jersey. I came in to do the night show and I peeked out through the curtain and the whole audience was women. So I asked Sam Cohen, the manager, 'What is that?' He said, 'Well, they work at the airplane factory and they were having this get-together and they decided all they wanted to do was to see you so they hired the whole theater.' Nothing but women, a sea of women."

After the war years and the continuous shutdown of burlesque theaters, the scene changed. As striptease moved into nightclubs and orchestras and comedians became scarce, shows focused solely on the stripping. Queens were pressured to flash to appease male audience members who wanted more bang for their buck. Lois said there were "only two jobs I ever walked out on, at the Zebra and the Empire Theater in Newark. The boss got fresh at the Zebra. And at the Empire Theater, Meyers, who was the manager of the theater, came back and told me, he says, 'You know, you could work stronger.' I said, 'I don't work any stronger.' He said, 'Well, we have those little red lights in the pit when the cops are in. When the lights are off, you can do anything you want.' I said, 'But I don't do anything else.' And he said, 'Well, you know . . . ' And I said, 'I'm not even shaved.' And he sent me a razor back the next show. So I left."

Lois had another bad experience in a nightclub that convinced her it was time to leave the business. She told me that it was starting to get seedy and she didn't think she was up for the compromises she was expected to make. Pressing her on what kind of advances were made, she told me, "Well, when an owner of a nightclub tells you he wants you to sit with the captain of police and you say you don't want to sit with the captain of police and he more or less tells you that he can hire four or five Puerto Rican girls for the salary he's paying you and you tell him, 'Well, go ahead and do it,' and you walk out. That's how it was getting seedy." Lois left the stage in 1959, calling it her "bow out." Her take on contemporary strippers is this: "Modern day girls are nude, lewd, and get screwed."

ois says, "[As] a star act, honey, you paid for your music, you paid pictures, you paid your press agent, you paid your traveling expenses, your hotel expenses, your costumes. They [the management] didn't pay for anything. They just gave you your salary and you were on your own."

519

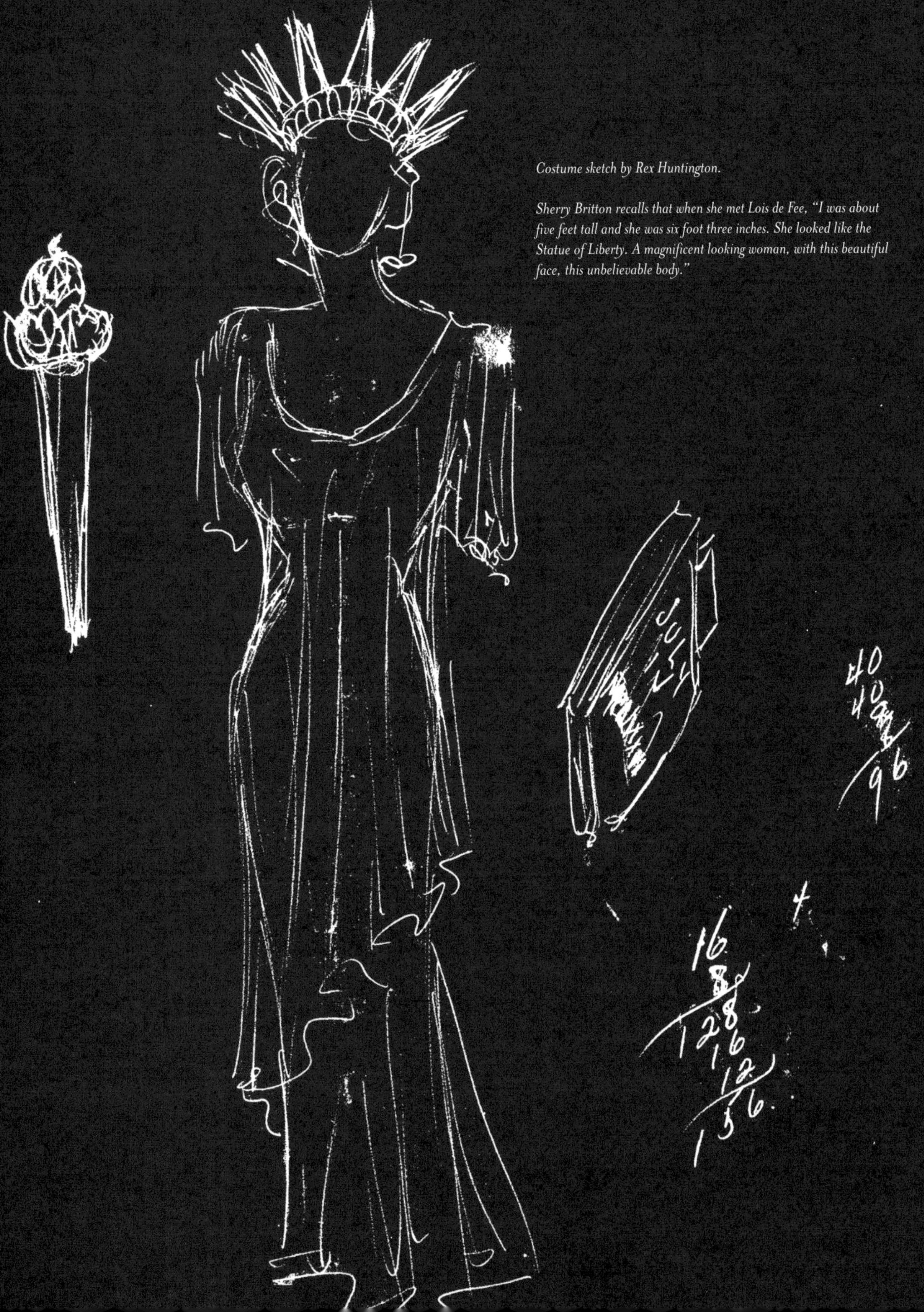

Costume sketch by Rex Huntington.

Sherry Britton recalls that when she met Lois de Fee, "I was about five feet tall and she was six foot three inches. She looked like the Statue of Liberty. A magnificent looking woman, with this beautiful face, this unbelievable body."

1947

Lois with her daughter Star.

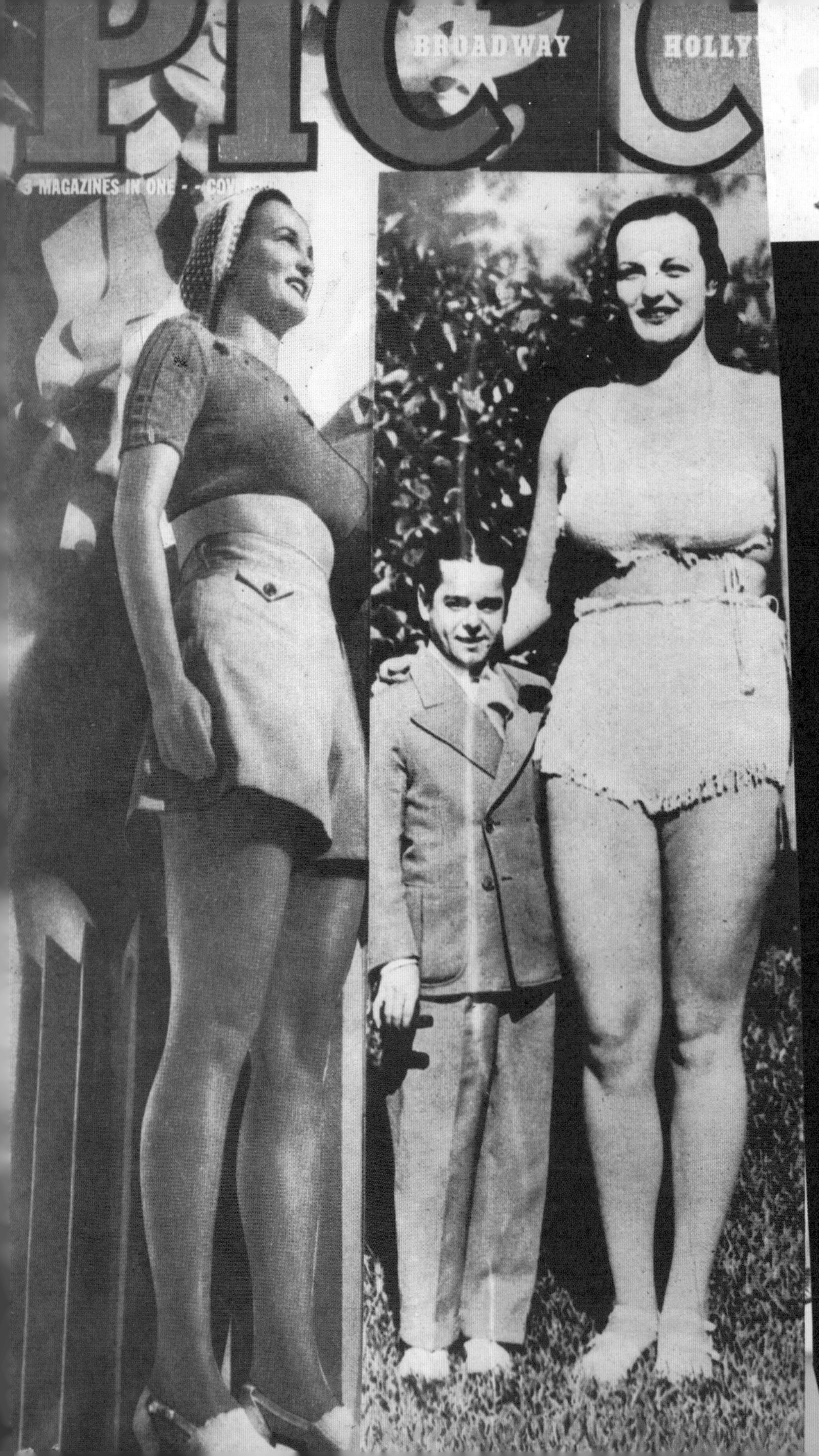

The Toni Twins on Lois:

JOAN: She was a monster. She was very big, tall. Married a midget.

MARIE: She was an Amazon.

ZORITA ON LOIS:
She was married seven times I think—six or seven times—and one of those times she got married, she married this midget for publicity—no reason. She never went to bed with him, I'm sure.

Police off.
Dinner 1947

So What's new?
Ch. Sam
1947

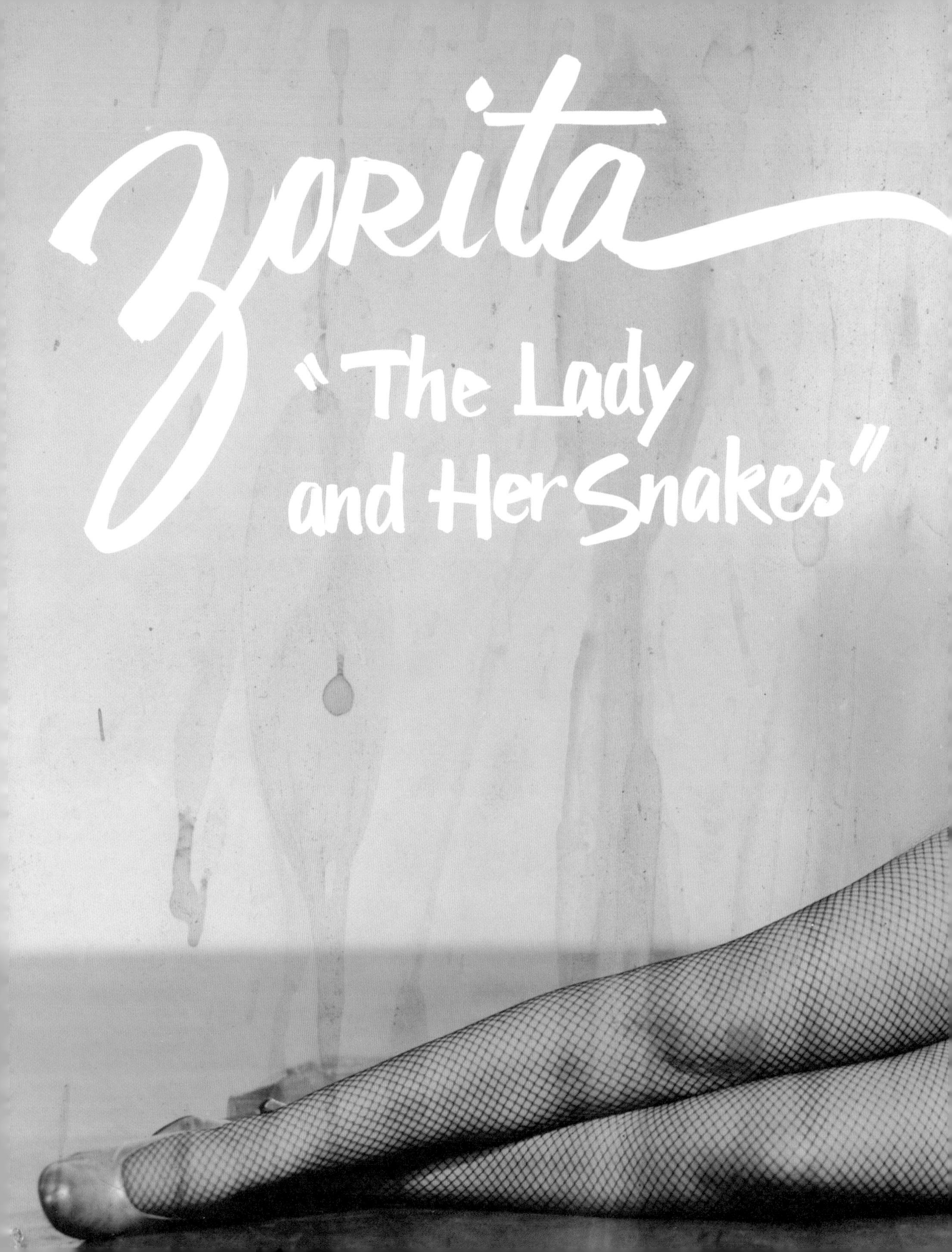
Zorita
"The Lady
and Her Snakes"

Murray
Korman
N.Y.

Sherry Britton was the first person to mention Zorita's name to me. Sherry counted her among the few headlining stars (beside herself and Lois de Fee) with whom she remained close and considered legendary. Sherry gave me Zorita's address and phone number and instructed me to call her by her stage name only. As Zorita (a.k.a. Ada Petillo) later told me, "Nobody calls me Ada but my mother and the FBI."

Newspaper advertisement for Zorita's show at the Victory.

Zorita is a true broad if I've ever met one—and believe me, I've met a few. We began corresponding through letters (she signed her letters with a snakehead turning into a "Z") and phone calls. She gave me strict orders never to call between 7 and 8 P.M., as she would be watching her favorite television show, *Jeopardy*. She had retired on five acres in Florida, purchased with income from General Motors' stock. The first time we spoke, she told me that she would never "shack up" with anyone unless they gave her stock shares in return.

Zorita was born in Ohio and adopted by a Methodist family when she was nine months old. She said that the preacher in town knew "a newly married woman who had tried to have a child and couldn't. He suggested that she see me, and she liked me and I was the cutest little bastard in the orphanage." Relatives told her adoptive mother, "You've got to watch that child, she's got bad blood," referring to Zorita's birth mother. Zorita said the only thing she was told about her biological mother was that she "was dragged out into the street by a dog on a chain and was killed." Zorita's problems at home first erupted when her adopted mother married her second husband, who liked Zorita "too well." Zorita was itching to leave home and finally did at age fifteen by marrying an Englishman in the civil service and moving with him to Chicago.

Zorita said in total she was married to "an Englishman, a Jew, and

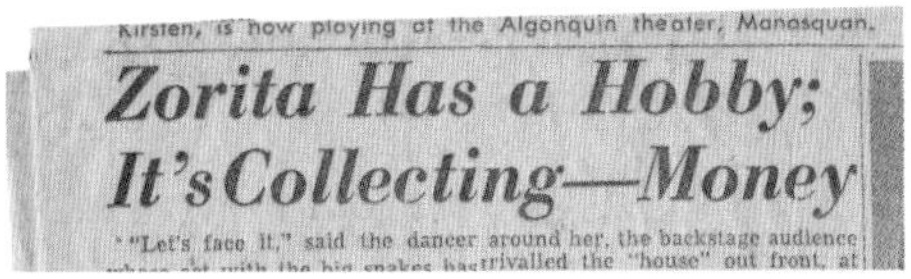
Kirsten, is now playing at the Algonquin theater, Manasquan.

Zorita Has a Hobby; It's Collecting—Money

"Let's face it," said the dancer around her, the backstage audience

Regarding her love for striking a good deal, Zorita once told me, "I don't part with ice in winter."

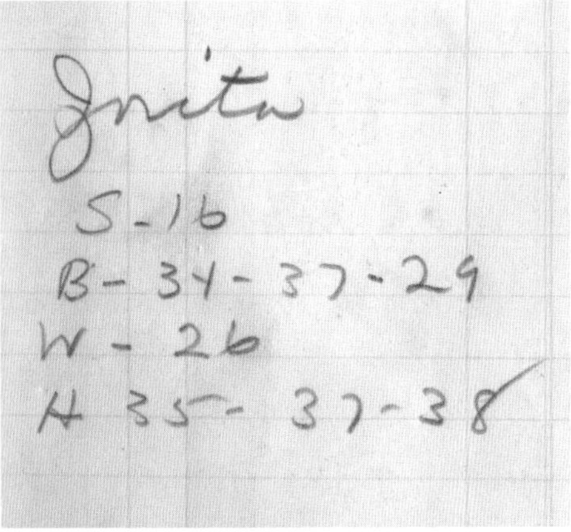

Zorita's measurements from Rex Huntington's notebook.

a wop—and I auditioned a few friends in between." Sherry Britton said she never knew or met any of Zorita's husbands—apparently they weren't worth much mention in Zorita's book. Zorita didn't like her first husband (they were married for only five weeks) and wanted to get out of the house, so she got a job manicuring in a barbershop run by "boys from the racket." Soon one of the boys asked her if she would like to go out to a dinner party they were having at an athletic club. "And so, I went to dinner with them, and there must have been forty girls and forty guys there. And, one of the girls was a southern girl, Junie Baby, and she took a fancy to me and invited me over to her apartment the next couple of days. I didn't have any decent clothes, and she gave me some very lovely clothes and things, and I wound up paying for them in a roundabout way." When I asked her how exactly she paid for them, she answered, "I ain't telling you."

Zorita told me that she found out when she was young and broke in Chicago what it meant to have to "pay" for favors. She mentioned a story about being sick and unable to work at the barbershop while living in a hotel room with overdue rent: "The owner of the hotel came around and said, 'Well, you owe us two week's hotel bill. You want to get laid?' And I said, 'No, I'll take care of it,' and I met a lawyer and I had him pay that hotel bill. And I thought, 'Nobody's ever going to proposition me [again].'"

Zorita was still—to use her own words—"fifteen years old with big knockers" when another woman she met invited her to a stag party given by a bachelor. She took Zorita under her wing and taught her how to strip. Paid fifteen dollars apiece for doing two or three parties a night, Zorita brought her own phonograph machine or an accordion player with her for accompaniment, though she remarks, "It's hell trying to dance to an accordion." Interestingly, she took off more during a stag party than she ever did on a burlesque stage because stag strippers performed completely nude, with groups of rowdy men attempting to grab at them. Zorita never worked legionnaire affairs, saying they were too rough. She wore a belt around her waist made of rope, and if anyone came too close, she would whip him. She didn't like men's hands on her and found their hairy chests "repulsive."

Zorita moved on to greener pastures after one of the stag party attendees took a shine to her talents and got her a job working at the San Diego World's Fair. She debuted as "Miss England" in a nudist colony exhibition. This entailed walking around in the freezing cold and parading her "country's delights," accompanied by old men with long beards wearing jock straps to give it a little atmosphere. Also on the bill at the fair was "Geek," a carnival performer who bit the heads off of live chickens and charmed snakes. At once attracted to and repulsed by his animals, Zorita befriended the Geek. As a parting gift, he gave her two snakes, Elmer and Oscar, which she kept in a canvas sack in her closet. At the fair Zorita met another man who owned the Capital Theater in San Francisco. He persuaded her to join his burlesque troupe there, to replace a girl who performed under the name "Sarita," which was then changed to "Zorita."

Appearing onstage in a *legitimate* production was a big step up for Zorita, and since she was the owner's girlfriend, everyone catered to her, which didn't hurt her enthusiasm for her newfound profession. The producer of the show taught Zorita to dance—her first serious lessons. Each show would run for two weeks and then the acts changed. She wanted to do an act that told a story: "So I says to this faggot producer—I got two snakes in my closet in my hotel" and came up with a number called "Consummation of the Wedding of the Snake." In the act, a gorgeous young maiden is going to be sold into slavery to an ugly old man. Instead she dances with a snake, gets bitten, and dies. (Unconsciously, she was adopting the Shakespearean double entendre, by which the word "die" doubles for "orgasm.") Zorita reenacted the number for me in a step-by-step monologue, replete with grinding and orgasmic moans as the wedding reaches its "consummation." Her act was a grand success, causing instant acclaim and controversy. Soon Zorita was racking up inches in Walter Winchell's column, consorting with Orson Welles, and showing Lana Turner her snakes' charms.

Zorita's reputation as an "out" lesbian since the late 1930s was unusual for the time, and for her profession. While she made the boys go wild onstage, she received a mixed reaction from her colleagues offstage. Even the Toni Twins, upon first hearing her name during an interview, commented on her sexuality as a defining characteristic, along with her snake routine. Zorita's camaraderie with the women who performed on the same bill was dicey at best. She was, after all, the star, and her brassy behavior was sure to ruffle a few feathers. She said that other queens often assumed that she was making a pass at them when she simply wanted some friendly company. She told me, "Once in a while, I didn't want to eat alone and I'd go into a restaurant and maybe there'd be a girl from the theater there. And I'd pick up her

Zorita headlines at the Piccadilly Club in Miami.

dinner check, just to avoid eating alone. And I found out that when I picked up their dinner checks, they decided that you were making a pass at them. And so I stopped doing that. They went back into the dressing room and said, 'You'll never guess who picked up my dinner check: Zorita.' 'Umm. Oh, did she make a pass at you?' 'No, she didn't make a pass at me, but maybe she's working up to it.' I wasn't working up to anything."

Zorita certainly didn't lack for female company. She kept a scrapbook, which she referred to as her "dyke book," in which there are countless photographs of her conquests: beautiful women posed on fur rugs, in front of Christmas trees, and on Zorita's bed. There are also photos of her at chic nightspots with other well-known bisexuals and lesbians of the film and theater worlds, including Martha Raye and Marlene Dietrich. Zorita's open attitude about her sexuality did not sit well with theater owners, who wanted her to maintain her sex goddess status offstage as well: "One time I came out of the Empire Theater, and the three owners of the theater were standing there. I came out in a butchy suit like this [points to a scrapbook photo of her in masculine street attire] and they said to me, 'Do you have to come out dressed like that by the stage door?' I said, 'Look, when I'm on your stage, I wear nineteen thousand ruffles. I do my act. When I come out on my own time, I wear what I want to. If you don't like it, kiss this.'"

Regardless of her sexual preference, Zorita was well aware of how to push the envelope and drive both men and women wild with expectation. I once asked Zorita if she ever flashed, knowing the answer before the question escaped my lips. When she replied in the affirmative, I wondered aloud if it was for the extra applause. She said it got your "name known more. . . . You flashed all the time, as much as you could. Everybody had their own system and style. I had elastic on my G-strings that I could pull between my legs and pull it way up, but if I saw that the police were in I could just spread my legs and the G-string would pop right back up and cover me, and I was home free." Sherry Britton, commenting further on Zorita's inventiveness, told me that Zorita customized a fox fur G-string by shaving it down the middle and dying it to match her hair, so it resembled pubic hair. "She had different color G-strings [for different hair colors]." Zorita recounted an incident in Toledo, Ohio, where she was arrested for flashing. She claimed this to be a false charge as she had seen the cops on her way in the club. "Knowing they're in, wouldn't I be stupid to flash? And they busted me for . . . flashing. And they said that they could see hair. I said, 'That's impossible, I haven't had a hair on my knish in years.'"

Zorita gave me a thorough schooling in the art of handling men. She operated on the premise that men are out to get the most they can from you, and give the least in return. Therefore, the tables must be turned. For example, if a man wants to take you out to dinner, the least he could do is pony up $500. "Well, little girls need new shoes, baby needs new shoes," Zorita said. Sherry claims that Zorita was a "call girl and accumulated a great fortune. She's living on this lovely estate in Florida and very comfortable. But she was quite candid about it and quite casual about it. I couldn't have been. She called me backstage and she said, 'Would like to turn a trick?' And I said, 'What does that mean?' And when she explained to me, I said, 'Oh my God, no.' She said, 'You mean, you're giving a million dollars worth of it away?' She was outraged to think that I was doing it for nothing and not profiting as she was, you know?" The line between burlesque striptease and "turning tricks" was blurred for Zorita—but she was no common prostitute. I prefer to think of Zorita as a modern courtesan.

Zorita recounted for me her liaisons with big businessmen and VIPs: "When I think of all the senators I've had affairs with and never made a big deal out of, I could throw up." One congressman from West Virginia gave her a red fox jacket to keep her warm at night when he couldn't. He even had a bricklayer build her entire house without even a promise of a dinner alone with her. Zorita once sent me an old two-page typed fan letter from a gentleman requesting a rendezvous. He wrote, "Candy is eaten quickly, flowers wither overnight. Replique perfume I'm not familiar with. But no matter. To me, it seems very likely that should we meet, we could iron out any uncertain details in a matter of minutes. . . . If that is convenient for you, we might be able to set something up that would be mutually pleasant and profitable in a variety of ways."

The appeal of burlesque performance and the key to a stripper's control is the element of tease—the audience can look but cannot touch. Zorita explained that it was part of the fun to give "everybody a hard-on and they can't have it," and she told me to be flattered to think that I, too, could have the power to give them a "hard-on." She said she found out at an early age that "sex could be paid for. And so you give them a peek, you give them a flash, you give them a smell but you don't give it all." I assumed that she was referring to her "hotel bill" story, but she elaborated further: "I learned it from early, very early childhood . . . [the] lady that adopted me had a brother who was gay and he had different guys in the house and the guys would make a move for me. So I moved out of the way. Unless I tried to chisel them for cigarettes or something. I didn't know how to smoke but somebody gave me a cigarette holder and I liked to burn myself [with it]." It is no surprise, hearing her talk, how she cultivated her opinion of men and her desire to profit from them. She once told me, "What is there to like? Hairy chests? A limp joint? You like them because they're customers, because they admire you, because they applaud, because they spend their money to see you."

In the early 1950s, Zorita had a child with her second husband, Pete Petillo ("the wop"). The marriage didn't last long, as Zorita wanted to get back to work. She took her daughter to the theater with her, adjusting her routine to include a new baby. She was working at the Onyx Club on Fifty-second Street in New York and used a private apartment upstairs as her dressing room. She continued to headline in New York, Chicago, Boston, and Baltimore and across the country, making around $1,800 a week (a huge salary then), shocking audiences and causing trouble wherever she went.

Zorita names Sherry Britton, Margie Hart, Lois de Fee, Betty Rowland, and herself as the only surviving authorities to speak as "burlesque queens." They were the last headlining stars before Mayor La Guardia started his campaign against burlesque in New York. In 1939 he outlawed the use of the word "burlesque" and closed down several theaters (including Minsky's). Thus, the era of the nightclub began. The strip became its own entity, as the big burlesque production numbers faded out.

I asked Zorita if she thought contemporary strip clubs could be considered "burlesque." She called these clubs "trash," adding that girls now have to perform for men who aren't interested in wardrobe or music—just stuffing tips in dancers' bras and G-strings. In burlesque theaters, customers were never allowed to offer cash to the performers, at least not onstage. Even throwing coins was rare, and only happened with a rough audience. Zorita said, "One time, at the Hudson Theater in Union City on a Saturday night, I was warned when I opened that theater. They said, 'Watch out for Saturday nights—the late show.' You did a fourth show, or a third show, on Saturday night, which was a midnight show, and it was a rough audience—very rough. 'Come on, kid, take it off. Hey, hey.' So, I went up to do my number, and in the middle of my number some guy was flipping coins out on the stage, and those coins hit you. They hurt. So, I said, 'Just a minute. Give me a house light. I am here to entertain you and amuse you, not be insulted by you. Now, I am not insulted if you throw money at me . . . but if you want to throw money, throw it wrapped around a dollar bill or a fifty- or one hundred-dollar bill . . . and I'll accept it. If you throw money, throw it the way I want it thrown.'"

As the saying goes, if you can't beat 'em, join 'em. So when Zorita retired from the stage in the early 1960s, she opened up several of her own nightclubs. The most successful was a club in Miami called Zorita's Showbar, which she ran with her business partner, Monique, ex-wife of burlesque theater owner Leroy Griffith. Zorita produced an annotated "burlesque" show, and Monique showed dirty movies. However liberal Zorita was, she would not come into the club when her partner booked Linda "Deep Throat" Lovelace because she felt it was immoral. Lovelace, who died in 2002, was one of the first porn stars, known for her starring role as a woman whose sexual organs were located in her throat.

After she retired from the stage, Zorita was the MC and impresario of her own burlesque club, Zorita's Show Bar.

Zorita was proud of the girls she cultivated to perform in her club. There were between ten and twelve dancers at any given time during the twelve-year run of the Showbar. Zorita sent me photographs and clippings—some with notes attached—of the dancers. There is Marlene, who married a millionaire; T.T. Red, whose contortionist nude act Zorita called "disgusting"; and "Puerto Rican Baby Doll," a young protégé of Zorita's who committed suicide while under Zorita's roof. Zorita's criteria for choosing her girls included a good bust. She prided herself on personally training them and fixing them up with an appropriate wardrobe, which was a must for Zorita. As emcee of the Showbar, Zorita worked fully clothed for the first time, microphone in hand. There were two rows of benches in the middle of the room, and a long bar that doubled as a stage. Zorita said she would only seat men at the bar because her girls felt uncomfortable working directly in front of women. One of the scenes from Bob Fosse's *Lenny* features Zorita working as an emcee, as her Showbar gained local notoriety.

Zorita spoke of her career in burlesque with pride but was not particularly nostalgic for days long past. She kept her many scrapbooks on the shelf and told me that until I asked her to pull them out, she hadn't looked at them in years. She said "Wouldn't you hate to live with somebody that was so hung up on oneself that they were busy looking at scrapbooks all day long and telling you what a great act they were? I know I was good."

When Margie Hart passed away in January 2000, I called Zorita to tell her. She was sad to hear the news and she said I needed to "hurry" with my research, as "the ladies are almost all gone." Several months later, Zorita went into the hospital with a broken hip. She was kicked out of the convalescence home (according to her) for harassing the nurses and causing trouble . . . good ol' Zorita. For the next six months, we wrote and spoke on the phone regularly, though with all the pain medication she was taking, she found it hard to speak for long or remember things clearly. She hoped I got everything I could from her memories, certain she would not be lucid for much longer. Her famous edge was fading fast, though she kept hanging on, maintaining her "tough broad" exterior. The final line of Zorita's last letter to me reads, "Stay away from tall buildings"—dated September 10, 2001. I had been living two blocks from the World Trade Center and had been displaced from my apartment on September 11. I made a phone call to tell her I was alright (all my burlesque queen friends had called or written expressing love and concern). We spoke briefly about my immediate situation. This conversation was to be our last. A month later she was gone.

I was stunned and frustrated. I never had the chance to say goodbye, to tell her how much of an inspiration she was to me, or to show her the life story I had been recording of her and her colleagues. It wasn't possible her light had gone out—she was too proud, too strong. When I called Lois de Fee to give her the news, she didn't believe that "Zo" could be gone, saying she was too "alive and spirited" to pass. Sherry Britton also had trouble reconciling the loss of Zorita: "I felt we'd kind of go on to eternity together."

When I told Sherry how much I admired her and Zorita, and how much I wanted to be like them, Sherry pushed me, asking what exactly I wanted to learn from their lessons. I told her that I guessed I wanted a little bit of their beauty and spirit to rub off on me. Zorita had blown my hypothesis on burlesque queens to bits. I had been keeping my research at arm's length, unsullied by any seedy reality, refusing to desecrate my own image of the glamorous burlesque queen. She confronted my theories and allowed me to recognize the flaws in my romanticizing of burlesque, for which I will be forever grateful. Zorita showed me that my fantasies would be enriched and become more poignant in light of the truths that lay in the shadows. I am just starting to adopt her lessons of self-empowerment and my confidence has grown stronger in the wake of our friendship. Though I may not use my body to get my way, I now understand how to tailor her philosophies to suit my own ambitions. I will always remember Zorita as the glamorous, mythical figure she was, whose life history illustrates the complexities of the last great burlesque queens.

Newspaper advertisement for Zorita's starring role in the B movie, I Married a Savage.

Man I bought
Snakes from

SHERRY BRITTON: She tied [the snakes] up and wouldn't let them go to the bathroom.

LIZ: Did she?

SHERRY BRITTON: Yeah, because the first time she used one it splished all over her and the chorus girls. So, from then on she taped it, until it died, and she'd get a new one from Texas.

LIZ: She taped it around the mouth?

SHERRY BRITTON: No, no, no, around wherever it ex—does its duty from.

I had a big girl show on a
Carnival - The World of
Mirth - This was
taken back stage
Elmer + Me

Murray Korman
N.Y.

Murray
Korman
N.Y.

"ZORITA"

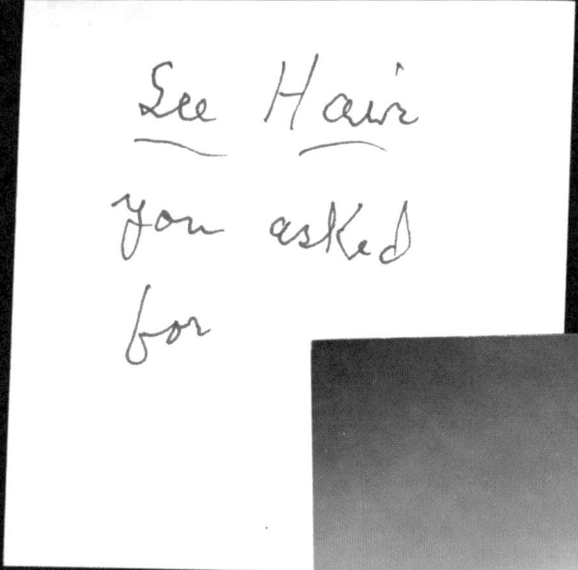
See Hair you asked for

PREVIOUS PAGE:
Zorita pictured in her bride and groom number. Zorita was known for her creative and outrageous routines, including a spiderweb act where a spider stripped her of her costume. Of another number, she said, "I did a number with this boy dressed in a gorilla suit. It was a beauty and the beast thing."

Murray Korman
N.Y.

Fin

ACKNOWLEDGMENTS

Special thanks to Judith Regan, Anna Bliss and Richard Ljoenes at Regan Books; for design assistance, Stuart Smith and Cassandra Kegler; calligraphy by Bonnie Nelson, Bambi the Pocket-Sized Venus, Marie Bradley, Sherry Britton, Red Buttons, Camille 2000, Richard Collier, Hope Diamond, Lois de Fee, Dixie Evans, Stacey Farrell, Jeanine Wedmore France, Leroy Griffiths, Gussie Gross, Ruthie Lewis, Rozanne McAllister, Fayard Nicolas, Nocturn, Flame O'Neill, Betty Rowland, Patti Starr, Joan Torino, Dolores Albin, Andy Davis, Kathe Green, Dr. William Green, Nils Hanson, Helen Hastings, Kurt and Rhonda Heinzinger, Stéphane Houy-Towner, Stephanie Iverson, Miles Kreuger, Tony Kriss, Michael Lear, Kady Lane, Wade Laboissoniere, John Lahr, Sara Murphy, Katherine O'Brien, Erik Preminger, Beverly Robinson, Dr. David S. Shields, Bob Taylor, Peter Thomas, Lane Willingham, Rob Zalkind, Richard Ziegfeld, Academy of Motion Picture Arts and Sciences Library, Exotic World, Motion Picture & Television Fund Retirement Community, New York Public Library for the Performing Arts, Billy Rose Theater Collection, Velvet Hammer, and The Ziegfeld Club.

SELECTED BIBLIOGRAPHY

Personal interviews by Liz Goldwyn with: Delores Albin, Athena the Grecian Siren of Sex, Bambi the Pocket-Sized Venus, Marie Bradley, Sherry Britton, Red Buttons, Richard Collier, Andrew Davis, Lois de Fee, Hope Diamond, Dixie Evans, Stacey Farrell, Ray Fisher, Jeanine Wedmore France, Dr. William Green, Gussie Gross, Nils Hanson, Margie Hart, Miles Krueger, Wade Laboissoniere, John Lahr, Ruthie Lewis, Rozanne McAllister, Anita Middleton, Sara Murphy, Fayard Nicolas, Nocturn, Flame O'Neill, Erik Preminger, Beverly Robinson, Betty Rowland, Patti Starr, Tanayo, Bob Taylor, Peter Thomas, Zorita.

Ackroyd, Peter. *Transvestitism and Drag: The History of an Obsession.* New York: Simon and Schuster, 1979.

Allen, Ralph G. "Burlesque." *American Heritage.* June/July 2002, 49–56.

Allen, Robert C. *Horrible Prettiness: Burlesque and American Culture.* Chapel Hill: University of North Carolina Press, 1991.

Appignanesi, Lisa. *The Cabaret.* London: Studio Vista, 1975.

Baker, Josephine and Jo Bouillon. *Josephine.* New York: Harper & Row, 1977.

Bentley, Toni. *Costumes by Karinska.* New York: Harry N. Abrams, 1995.

Blatchford, William (editor). *The Memoirs of Cora Pearl: The Erotic Reminiscences of a Flamboyant 19th Century Courtesan.* London: Granada, 1983.

Blessing, Jennifer. *Rrose is a Rrose is a Rrose: Gender Performance in Photography.* New York: Guggenheim Museum, 1997.

Brooks, Louise. *Lulu in Hollywood.* New York: Alfred A. Knopf, 1974.

Calasibetta, Charlotte Mankey, Ph.D. *Fairchild's Dictionary of Fashion, 2nd Edition.* New York: Fairchild, 1988.

Corio, Ann with Joseph DiMona. *This Was Burlesque.* New York: Madison Square Press, Grosset & Dunlap, 1968.

De Mille, Agnes. *America Dances.* New York: Macmillian, 1980.

De Pougy, Liane. *My Blue Notebooks.* New York: Harper & Row, 1979.

Holliday, Robert Cortes. *Unmentionables: From Figleaves to Scanties.* New York: Ray Long & Richard R. Smith, 1933.

Knight, Arthur and Hollis Alpert. "The History of Sex in Cinema, Part Six: The Thirties—Censorship and the Depression." *Playboy,* November 1965, pp. 150–157, 208–221.

Kochno, Boris. *Diaghilev and the Ballets Russes.* New York: Harper & Row, 1970.

Lartigue, Jacques-Henri. *Les Femmes Aux Cigarettes.* New York: Viking Press, 1980.

Laver, James. *Clothes.* London: Burke, 1952.

——. *Costume in Theater.* New York: Hill and Wang, 1964.

——. *Modesty in Dress.* Boston: Houghton Mifflin Company, 1969.

Lavine, Robert W. *In a Glamorous Fashion: The Fabulous Years of Hollywood Costume Design.* New York: Charles Scribner's Sons, 1980.

Lee, Gypsy Rose. *Gypsy: A Memoir by Gypsy Rose Lee.* New York: Dell, 1957.

Leese, Elizabeth. *Costume Design in the Movies.* New York: Dover Publications, Inc., 1991.

Lewis, Arthur J. *La Belle Otero.* New York: Trident Press, 1967.

Los Angeles County Museum of Art. *Hollywood and History: Costume Design in Film.* Los Angeles: Thames & Hudson, 1987.

McEvoy, J.P. *Showgirl.* New York: Simon & Schuster, 1928.

Prato, Museo Pucci. Exhibition catalog. "Fellini: Costumes and Fashion." Milan: Charta, 1996.

Preminger, Eric Lee. *Gypsy and Me.* Boston: Little, Brown, 1984.

Sert, Misia. *Misia & the Muses.* New York: John Day, 1953.

Sobel, Bernard. *A Pictorial History of Burlesque.* New York: G.P. Putnam's Sons, 1956.

Steele, Valerie. *Fashion and Eroticism.* New York: Oxford University Press, 1985.

Vertes, Marcel. *Art and Fashion.* New York: Studio Publications, 1944.

Vreeland, Diana. *D.V.* New York: Alfred A. Knopf, 1984.

Waldberg, Patrick. *Eros in La Belle Epoque.* New York: Grove Press, 1969.

West, Mae. *Goodness Had Nothing to Do with It.* New Jersey: Prentice-Hall, 1959.

Wortley, Richard. *A Pictorial History of Striptease.* London: Octopus Books, 1976.

Ziegfeld, Richard and Paulette. *The Ziegfeld Touch: The Life and Times of Florenz Ziegfeld Jr.* New York: Harry N. Abrams, 1993.

EPHEMERA AND PHOTOGRAPHY CREDITS

"Mopsy" by Gladys Parker: 25. Courtesy of the Picture Desk, Inc.: 32. "SALOME" ©1953, renewed 1981 Columbia Pictures Industries, Inc. All Rights Reserved. Courtesy of Columbia Pictures: 34. "Dance of the Doves" by Llewellyn: 141. Reprinted by permission of the Detroit Free Press: 149 (left). Ball of Fire © 1941, Samuel Goldwyn Jr. Family Trust. All Rights Reserved. Courtesy of MGM CLIP+STILL: 182, 183, 185. © Reprinted with permission of King Features/North America Syndicate: 75. Maurice Seymour / M. P. & T. V. Photo Archive: title page, 22, 23, 56, 129 (bottom). Billy Rose Theater Collection, The New York Public Library for the Performing Arts: 100, 101, 106, 107, 108, 109, 110, 113, 116, 117, 119 (4), 120 (5), 122, 123 (3).Collection of Joan Torino: Sketch by Rex Huntington: vi, 31 (right), 39, 49, 51, 55, 57, 58, 59, 60, 61, 62, 142, 249; Rex Huntington ledger: 44, 45, 52, 65, 143, 260 (bottom); Rex Huntington note paper: 54 (top and bottom left); Rex Huntington measurement form: 54; Rex Huntington notes: 67; Photos by Murillo, St. Louis: 9; Theatrical Chicago: 13 (2); Strand, NY: 14, 16 (2), 18, 66, 124, 279; Bert, K. F.: 15 (left); Bloom: 63; Garbo of Chicago: 82; Gene LaVerne of Buffalo, NY: 64; Boris Bakeny, NYC: 65; Hollywood Studio: 94 (bottom); Empire: 125; Murray Korman, NY: 133; Unidentified photographer: xv, 10, 15 (right), 38, 46, 47 (5), 48 (3), 52 (left and center), 53 (bottom right), 66 (Showbill cover), 94 (top), 102, 103, 104, 105, 126, 127, 128, 130, 131, 137, 140 (left), 158, 170, 171 (3), 218, 230. Collection of Liz Goldwyn: Photos by Hussein Katz: xii, xiv, xvi, xvii, 26, 27 (2), 28, 29 (2), 33, 70; Peter Stanglmayr: x; Liz Goldwyn: xiii (2); Jennifer Augustyn: xv; Unidentified photographer: xii, 19, 92, 93, 95, 112, 118, 121, 129 (top), 262, 268, 269, 270, 271; Murray Korman: 256, 257, 258, 272, 273, 274 (2), 275, 276, 277; Postcards: xviii, 5 (2); Cigarette Cards: 6 (4); "Burlesque Family Tree" by Cassandra Kegler: 20, 21; Mail order catalogue: 43 (2); Notes: 53, 132, 241 (2), 267, 275; Advertisements: 225, 231, 259, 260 (top); Poster: 239. Collection of Betty Rowland: Photos by Gussie Gross: 180 (4), 181; John E. Reed, Hollywood: viii, 36, 37, 172, 173, 174, 184, 186, 187, 200, 201; Van Valkenburg and Dressler: 156, 157, 164, 165; Whitestone Photo NY: 166; Cliff, Hollywood: 167 (right); Murray Korman: 177; Unidentified photographer: xiv, 98 (2), 99, 159, 167 (left), 168, 169, 175, 176, 179, 188 (2), 189 (2), 193, 196, 197 (2), 198, 199, 209, 210 (2), 211 (2), 213 (5), 214, 215, 216, 217 (3); Unidentified newspaper clippings: 190, 191, 192, 193 (2), 194 (5), 195, 202, 203, 204, 207, 212; Advertisements: 194 (2), 205, 206, 212 (6), 213 (2); letters: 208, 212, 214. Collection of Gussie Gross: Sketch by Gussie Gross: 31 (left), 41, 42, 78, 79, 83, 84, 86, 87, 88, 89, 145, 146, 151; Unidentified newspaper clippings: 40, 136; Advertisements: 83, 149 (right); Letter from Ricki Covette: 148; Letter from La Contessa: 152; Sketch by Dixie Evans: 154; Business card: 71. Photos by Gussie Gross: 89 (3), 154 (2), 155 (2); 35 (4), 68, 69 (6), 79 (3), 80 (5), 81 (4), 84, 146 (2); William C. Thomas: 135 (3), 138, 139, 162 (4), 163 (4); Unidentified photographer: 24, 71, 72 (2), 73, 76, 77 (2), 85, 87 (2), 90 (6), 91 (5), 134 (2), 136, 140 (right), 147, 150, 152, 153, 161 (2). Collection of Lane Willingham: Letter: 227; Unidentified photographer: 220, 221, 222, 224 (2), 227, 228 (2), 229 (2), 232, 233 (2), 234, 235. Collection of Lois de Fee: Photos by Cawell NY: 238; Unidentified photographer: 236, 237, 242, 245, 246, 247, 248, 250, 251, 252, 253, 254, 255.

INDEX

Page references in **bold** indicate photographs and/or photograph captions.

© LGoldwyn Films

LIZ GOLDWYN has worked in fashion, art, and photography since the age of sixteen. She has produced major fashion shows and art installations, helped establish the fashion department at Sotheby's New York, and was a global consultant for Shiseido America. A frequent contributor to national magazines, she is also a sought-after jewelry designer. Along with this book, her documentary film *Pretty Things,* which premiered on HBO, helped usher in the revival of interest in burlesque and the women who gave it life. Goldwyn lives in Los Angeles.

www.lgoldwynfilms.com